Cryptoeconomics, Fundamental Principles of Bitcoin, 2nd Edition
Copyright ©2020 Eric Voskuil
Version 1.2.1, Paperback

Publisher
Published in the United States by Eric Voskuil

Author
Eric Voskuil

Editor & Illustrator
James Chiang

ISBN: 978-1-7350608-2-8

9 781735   060828

Author

Eric Voskuil

Eric Voskuil is a major contributor to Libbitcoin[1], a free and open source high performance Bitcoin developer toolkit. Eric graduated from Rensselaer Polytechnic Institute[2] with a degree in Computer Science, selling his first start-up company, DesktopStandard[3], to Microsoft[4] and his second, BeyondTrust[5], to Veritas Capital[6]. He has worked in core Bitcoin development since early 2014 and speaks at conferences and meet-ups globally. He is also a serial entrepreneur, angel investor, martial artist, avid motorcyclist, world traveler, and former U.S. Navy[7] fighter pilot.

In early 2020 he held CryptoEcon[8] in Hanoi, the first conference dedicated to cryptoeconomic theory, co-founded the Libbitcoin Institute[9] to help finance core Bitcoin development and education, sponsored the first Bitbikers[10] ride across Northern Vietnam and published the first edition of *Cryptoeconomics*.

Reference

[1] https://libbitcoin.info
[2] https://rpi.edu
[3] http://desktopstandard.com
[4] https://microsoft.com
[5] https://beyondtrust.com
[6] https://veritascapital.com
[7] https://www.navy.mil
[8] https://cryptoecon.org
[9] https://libbitcoininstitute.org
[10] https://bitbikers.org

Editor & Illustrator
James Chiang

James is an open-source contributor to both Libbitcoin[1] and Bitcoin Core[2] projects. He read his first *Cryptoeconomics* chapter, the Dedicated Cost Principle[3], in early 2018 and began sketching visuals to support his study of the underlying principles. He is currently conducting research on the formal security of smart contracts. James is a PhD candidate in computer science at the Technical University of Denmark[4] and a former Jet Propulsion Lab aerospace engineer.

Reference

[1] https://libbitcoin.info
[2] https://bitcoincore.org
[3] Chapter: Dedicated Cost Principle
[4] https://www.dtu.dk/english

Acknowledgements

This project began as tweets[1] and then posts to the Libbitcoin[2] software repository wiki[3]. Eventually there was enough content and interest that I started getting requests for a book. Then came offers to translate. Finally **James Chiang** attempted publication. He nearly completed assembly of the first edition, including his own illustrations. His insightful questions caused me to rethink the Inflation Principle[4], which led to an important economic insight. Yet my constant additions and changes at the time made completion nearly impossible. Eventually James moved on to bigger things, but his work and illustrations inspired the eventual publication. I can't thank him enough.

Over the past year **Fabrizio Armani** has been working on an Italian translation. His feedback helped improve this edition. His discomfort with the Savings Relation[5] eventually caused me to scale back its conclusion. I've been fortunate to have him as a sounding board for this edition. I try to be my own strongest critic when attempting to demonstrate a cryptoeconomic conclusion. But James and Fabrizio have clearly demonstrated the value of working with another committed party.

Bitcoin began for me with Libbitcoin. As soon as I got started I flew to Spain to meet **Amir Taaki**. He had created the Libbitcoin community and led the project until his detour to Rojava[6]. He was exceedingly patient with me as I was recovering my C++ skills and learning the idiosyncrasies of Bitcoin. Libbitcoin is a special community within the Bitcoin universe of core development, and Amir deserves the credit for that. It was the

Reference

[1] https://twitter.com
[2] https://libbitcoin.info
[3] https://github.com/libbitcoin/libbitcoin-system/wiki/Cryptoeconomics
[4] Chapter: Inflation Principle
[5] Chapter: Savings Relation
[6] https://en.wikipedia.org/wiki/Amir_Taaki

attempt to reconcile the hype around Bitcoin with what I knew from my experience with it that led to *Cryptoeconomics*. Choices made in development relate directly to the economic underpinnings. We needed to explain what we were doing to ourselves and others. Ultimately his work and insights led to this work, so it was fitting and much appreciated that he agreed to provide the Foreword[1].

I often refer to **Phillip Mienk** as the smartest person I know. He was hired into a Microsoft[2] pool out of the prestigious University of Illinois, Urbana-Champaign Computer Science[3] doctorate program. I was building a new development team at the time. I wasn't keen on having to train the college hire that Microsoft had dumped in my lap. I quickly realized how lucky I was. When I left he joined me for a third startup, and on the day that closed he joined me on Libbitcoin. He's been an instrumental partner for the last decade, always able to go straight to the heart of the most complex issues. I'm grateful for his support during some tough times and ultimately for his contribution to this work.

Neill Miller somehow found Libbitcoin and has made major contributions to our wallet and server interface code, and has maintained our community servers for several years. **Kulpreet Singh** tracked me down at Baltic Honeybadger[4] 2019 and picked my brain on Libbitcoin. Since that time he's made major contributions to our database test suite and has continued to work on design improvements in the underlying store. Along with Phillip, Neill and Kulpreet have been the backbone of Libbitcoin. Without their support it wouldn't be possible for me to spend so much time writing words when I should be writing code[5].

Reference

[1] Chapter: Foreword
[2] https://microsoft.com
[3] https://cs.illinois.edu
[4] https://bh2019.hodlhodl.com
[5] https://www.activism.net/cypherpunk/manifesto.html

The Libbitcoin Institute[1] is the brainchild of **Thomas Pacchia**. Tom gathered myself and **Lucas Betschart** to form the organization for the purpose of raising money to fund Libbitcoin's free software[2] development and Bitcoin education. He did all of the tedious work required to obtain 501c3 status[3] with the IRS. To date the IRS has not obliged, but the Institute remains a vehicle for supporting work necessary to advance the value proposition[4] of Bitcoin. Tom and Lucas have been tremendous supporters and good friends.

The first edition of *Cryptoeconomics* was distributed only to attendees at CryptoEcon[5] 2020 in Hanoi. The intent was to quickly release online for sale, but life got in the way. The extras remain in a motorcycle shop on Tay Ho Street. But CryptoEcon, a project of the Libbitcoin Institute, helped spread the word. The contributions of HODL Capital[6] (via **Thomas Pacchia**) and Lemniscap[7] (via **Roderik van der Graaf**) made the conference possible. Tom sought me out at Building on Bitcoin[8] 2018 in Lisbon, and Roderik found me at Baltic Honeybadger 2019 in Riga. They took the initiative, and inspired me to complete the book for the conference.

The people who have contributed the most in terms of inspiring topics and constructive criticism of ideas are too many to include. They include conference and meetup organizers, podcast hosts, attendees and listeners, and the seemingly endless stream of Twitter commentors. I've discovered far more from investigating flawed ideas than from

Reference

[1] https://libbitcoininstitute.org

[2] https://en.wikipedia.org/wiki/Free_Software_Foundation

[3] https://www.irs.gov/charities-non-profits/charitable-organizations/exemption-requirements-501c3-organizations

[4] Chapter: Value Proposition

[5] https://cryptoecon.org

[6] https://www.hodl.capital

[7] https://lemniscap.com

[8] https://building-on-bitcoin.com

sound ones. Yet without also having occasional voices of support this type of thing is much harder to accomplish.

Finally, thank you to my friends and family for supporting me through a difficult time.

CONTENTS

Table of Contents

FOREWORD

Foreword

By Amir Taaki

Crypto-anarchy[1] is neither a strategy to impose a political hegemony nor discredit other possible attitudes or agendas. It is merely a set of concepts or ideas that can be used tactically to realize alternative modes of being. History is the result of human will and action, but this always occurs within a framework of convictions, belief and representation which provide meaning and direction to any given pursuit. In this way, crypto-anarchy seeks to arm the individual with powerful conceptual tools to construct their own creative visions.

Economics is important since it is the study of the fundamental mechanisms of human action and their consequences. Rational economics analyzes human activity while accepting knowledge limitations. From a simple set of assumptions, including that humans act[2] and prefer things sooner than later[3], theorems are derived using rules of inference[4]. The result is powerful, as it is necessarily true under the assumptions. The development of these theorems provides us with simple constructs we can use to compartmentalize and analyze more complex phenomena.

Cryptocurrency[5] emerged from crypto-anarchy and free market economics, but since then has outgrown its own roots and become a contemporary entity with peculiar

Reference

[1] https://en.wikipedia.org/wiki/Crypto-anarchism
[2] https://en.wikipedia.org/wiki/Action_axiom
[3] https://en.wikipedia.org/wiki/Time_preference
[4] https://en.wikipedia.org/wiki/Rule_of_inference
[5] https://en.wikipedia.org/wiki/Cryptocurrency

characteristics. This has forced us to revisit our own ideas and assumptions about how these disciplines interrelate. This new field of study is termed cryptoeconomics.

Cryptocurrencies such as Bitcoin represent money which is simultaneously global, uncensored, and open access for everybody, for the first time in human history. There are also great advances being made in anonymization technology, not only for cryptocurrency but for other financial instruments and human activity. Cryptocurrency is therefore a unique phenomenon with its own characteristics worthy of study.

The importance of economics lies in giving us a window to understand the activities of human beings. This means we can make plans about where to apply our resources and our technical knowledge. The current generation of crypto companies lack this strategic dimension and will not be prepared to take advantage of new geopolitical trends. Presently there is too much divergence in focus – the crypto industry is not selective enough.

Concepts from evolutionary theory can help us to predict which kind of organizational strategies will win-out in the longer term. For example, r/K-Selection Theory[1] explains that after major extinction events, the first organisms to occupy niches are the species with high numbers of young that mature quickly and have little investment of resources from the parents (r-selected)[2]. However, they are edged out by organisms over the longer term, which have fewer young that are better specialized for niches and take longer to mature (K-selected)[3]. These K-selected crypto-organisms are the ones that will be better adapted to take advantage of new economic niches that are opening up.

Reference

[1] https://en.wikipedia.org/wiki/R/K_selection_theory
[2] https://en.wikipedia.org/wiki/R/K_selection_theory#r-selection
[3] https://en.wikipedia.org/wiki/R/K_selection_theory#K-selection

Another hypothesis from evolutionary theory is the Red Queen hypothesis[1], which is that organisms are in a constant battle to evolve. That is, we must constantly adapt and evolve in a continually changing environment with ever-evolving actors.

We do this through the process of applying our knowledge to find patterns and build conceptual models, modifying those models in feedback to improve their accuracy or augment their underlying paradigms.

The current crop of crypto companies will die out soon enough. In their place, a new generation of organizations will emerge. These will be highly adaptive, attuned to geopolitical trends, and optimized for survival in a state of perpetual disequilibrium. To withstand such conditions, this new generation should be founded on a synthesis that combines the astuteness of crypto-economics and crypto-anarchy itself – which is at its core a simple doctrine: the motor of historical change is not simply technological innovation, but concepts, models and ideas that give us power over material reality.

My experience with Eric goes back to 2013 when we began working on Bitcoin system software[2] that was both fast and scalable. Eric is a top tier developer who single-handedly can do the work of an entire team to create production level software – a very rare skill. He also has a wide-ranging life experiencing, having flown jets for the U.S. Navy and started multiple successful companies. He combines intense practical knowledge with a strong theoretical underpinning and a deep interest and knowledge in politics and economics.

Eric's unique insights into fundamental concepts provide us with a vital framework to guide the future direction of the cryptoeconomics field. He rigorously applies rational

Reference

[1] https://en.wikipedia.org/wiki/Red_Queen_hypothesis
[2] https://github.com/libbitcoin

economic theory to cryptocurrency, and ventures beyond the financial to explain how human activity shapes this future.

PREFACE

Preface

This started as a way to avoid retyping the same ideas, 140 characters[1] at a time. In keeping with that environment, topics were as short as possible, and informal. I did not intend to write a book, and still could not. Most of the topics (including this one) were written on my phone, on a flight, train or in a coffee shop. Many are quick observations that arise from intimate knowledge of core Bitcoin code or long self-study and experience in various disciplines.

Over time topics began to interact, a necessary taxonomy erupted, and what had been a casual process of ad-hoc observation started to become work. **The topics are as short as possible and assume some knowledge of both Bitcoin and economics**. I made an honest effort to rationalize relations and terminology, but my focus remains on consistency[2] and expansion of understanding. Fortunately, others have come along to help with illustration, review and publication.

I have used the terms Catallactics[3] and Praxeology[4] to describe the underlying discipline. People also use the term Austrian Economics[5]. I find each of these unsatisfying, so have started referring to the discipline as "Rational Economics" (not to be confused with economic rationalism[6]), a system based entirely on deductive reasoning[7] from a set of axioms[8].

Reference

[1] https://en.wikipedia.org/wiki/Twitter
[2] https://en.wikipedia.org/wiki/Consistency
[3] https://en.wikipedia.org/wiki/Catallactics
[4] https://en.wikipedia.org/wiki/Praxeology
[5] https://en.wikipedia.org/wiki/Austrian_School
[6] https://en.wikipedia.org/wiki/Economic_rationalism
[7] https://en.wikipedia.org/wiki/Deductive_reasoning
[8] https://en.wikipedia.org/wiki/Axiom

It was Mises[1] who explicitly established a system of economics on a rational basis, yet this approach does not pervade the entire Austrian School (which predates Mises). Rothbard[2] adds rigor and clarity to Mises, deriving some important new conclusions. Yet Mises (as most humans) makes material errors[3], which are unfortunately carried forth by Rothbard. Other errors commonly amplified within the Austrian School are clear misinterpretations.

In each case where Mises errs, he is critiquing state fiat money[4]. In other words, he appears to sacrifice his objectivity to his passion. Yet his rational system, properly applied, easily exposes the errors. State money deserves critique, and Bitcoiners rarely miss an opportunity. Yet it deserves *accurate* critique; anything less is counterproductive. With correct analysis, specific relevant forces can be identified, both in monopoly fiat (e.g. Dollar) and in market fiat (e.g. Bitcoin). Such proper analysis can limit the waste of precious capital on irrational propositions[5].

A strictly rational process not only exposes errors, but also produces new and interesting discoveries[6] and simplifications[7], not just in Bitcoin but in economic theory generally. The topics form a graph, over which no total ordering seems appropriate. The table of contents is a poorly imposed order. While some attempt at progression has been made, I recommend reading the topics as they were written, as a curiosity.

Reference

[1] https://en.wikipedia.org/wiki/Ludwig_von_Mises
[2] https://en.wikipedia.org/wiki/Murray_Rothbard
[3] Chapter: Inflation Principle
[4] Chapter: Money Taxonomy
[5] Chapter: Full Reserve Fallacy
[6] Chapter: Censorship Resistance Property
[7] Chapter: Depreciation Principle

INTRODUCTION

Introduction

Do you think you know something about Bitcoin and Austrian Economics[1]? If so you may be ready for *Cryptoeconomics*. This is not a work for the uninitiated. It is not a narrative and is free of opinion. The content is dense – it does not repeat itself. It is not a contribution to the echo chamber, will not show you how to set up a wallet, the future price, or what to do.

Cryptoeconomics applies rational economic principles to Bitcoin, demonstrating flaws and unnecessary complexities in them, and in common understandings of Bitcoin. It will improve your understanding of both. Bitcoin requires a new, rigorous, and comprehensive discipline. **This is it.**

Bitcoin is something new. It seems to defy understanding. Has there ever been a fixed supply money? Is there another case of production cost varying directly with product price? Is there anything else with a competitive yet fixed rate of transactability? To see past the hype, understand the value proposition, security model, and economic behavior, this may be your only source.

Bitcoin is economics, technology, and security. Without incorporating all of these aspects, errors will be made. Economists, technologists, security experts, and even numerologists[2] have attempted to explain it. Each brings a limited perspective, failing to incorporate essential aspects. The author found himself uniquely qualified to integrate them.

His work in Bitcoin began with a hardware wallet. He spent a year analyzing threats, working with electronics design, hardware exploitation, and state surveillance experts.

Reference

[1] https://en.wikipedia.org/wiki/Austrian_School
[2] https://twitter.com/100trillionusd

He chose the Libbitcoin[1] software library, as Satoshi's prototype was not factored for development and was largely financed by the Bitcoin Foundation[2], a corporate consortium. He later dedicated himself to Libbitcoin, eventually writing or editing all of its ~500,000 lines of code. Few have comparable experience with such a comprehensive Bitcoin stack.

As a combat-experienced fighter pilot in the U.S. Navy[3] he experienced state threats. He became a highly-qualified Strike Fighter Tactics Instructor[4], in which his primary role was tactics analysis and threat presentation. He also advised for the Navy on the Strike Fighter Training System[5] network, Joint Strike Fighter[6], early GPS weapons[7], and F/A-18[8] systems. His understanding of the physical nature of all security was enhanced by decades of training in Japanese martial arts, achieving black belt rankings in five disciplines.

His degree[9] and experience in computer science mixed with extensive business experience, founding several companies. He has worked at IBM[10] and as a Principal Architect at Microsoft[11], two of the world's largest companies. The latter purchased his first startup, and his second was acquired by Veritas Capital[12]. He was awarded three

Reference

[1] https://libbitcoin.info
[2] https://bitcoinfoundation.org
[3] https://www.navy.mil
[4] https://en.wikipedia.org/wiki/United_States_Navy_Strike_Fighter_Tactics_Instructor_program
[5] https://www.globalsecurity.org/military/library/policy/navy/ntsp/SFTS.htm
[6] https://en.wikipedia.org/wiki/Joint_Strike_Fighter_program
[7] https://en.wikipedia.org/wiki/Guided_bomb#Satellite
[8] https://en.wikipedia.org/wiki/McDonnell_Douglas_F/A-18_Hornet
[9] https://www.rpi.edu
[10] https://ibm.com
[11] https://microsoft.com
[12] https://www.veritascapital.com

related U.S. patents[1]. Eventually he became an angel investor, sharing his experience with other entrepreneurs.

As CTO[2] of his first company he published three computer security advisories via Computer Emergency Response Team[3]. Each was derived entirely from his reading of user documentation. Later he earned a seat on the DHS[4] Open Vulnerability Assessment Language[5] advisory board for his work on software patching. In recent years he uncovered material security flaws in each of the first three iterations of a popular "secure element" hardware wallet, again from review of user documentation.

Thirty years of self-study in free market economics was reinforced by extensive global travel. In visiting over 80 countries he has interacted with people on five continents. Still often traveling on a motorcycle with only a shoulder bag, he obtains intimate understanding of global economic realities. From Zimbabwean black market currency traders, to Tanzanian coffee pickers, Venezuelan refugees, Mongolian shepherds, Okinawan jazz musicians, Lao monks, etc. – the world is not as often presented.

The ability to integrate these diverse and relevant experiences led to *Cryptoeconomics*. This is your next stop.

Reference

[1] https://www.uspto.gov
[2] https://en.wikipedia.org/wiki/Chief_technology_officer
[3] https://en.wikipedia.org/wiki/CERT_Coordination_Center
[4] https://dhs.gov
[5] https://oval.cisecurity.org

SECURITY MODEL

Axiom of Resistance

In modern logic an axiom[1] is a premise, it cannot be proven. It is a starting assumption against which other things may be proven. For example, in Euclidean geometry[2] one cannot prove that parallel lines never meet. It simply defines the particular geometry.

Proving statements about Bitcoin requires reliance on axiomatic systems, specifically mathematics[3], probability[4] and catallactics[5], and therefore the assumptions upon which they rely. However Bitcoin also relies on an axiom not found in these systems.

Satoshi alludes to this in an early statement[6]:

> >You will not find a solution to political problems in cryptography.
>
> Yes, but we can win a major battle in the arms race and gain a new territory of freedom for several years.
>
> Governments are good at cutting off the heads of a centrally controlled networks like Napster, but pure P2P networks like Gnutella and Tor seem to be holding their own.
>
> *Satoshi Thu Nov 6 15:15:40 EST 2008*

In other words, there is an assumption that it is *possible* for a system to resist state control. This is not accepted as a fact but deemed to be a reasonable assumption, due to the behavior of similar systems, on which to base the system.

Reference

[1] https://en.wikipedia.org/wiki/Axiom
[2] https://en.wikipedia.org/wiki/Euclidean_geometry
[3] https://en.wikipedia.org/wiki/Zermelo%E2%80%93Fraenkel_set_theory
[4] https://en.wikipedia.org/wiki/Probability_axioms
[5] https://en.wikipedia.org/wiki/Catallactics
[6] http://satoshi.nakamotoinstitute.org/emails/cryptography/4

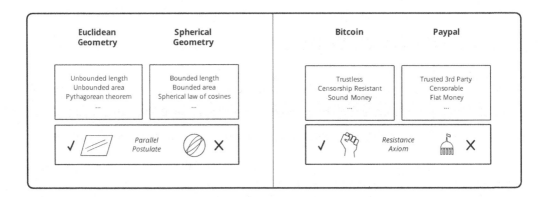

One who does not accept the axiom of resistance is contemplating an entirely different system than Bitcoin. If one assumes it is *not possible* for a system to resist state controls, conclusions do not make sense in the context of Bitcoin – just as conclusions in spherical geometry[1] contradict Euclidean. How can Bitcoin be permissionless[2] or censorship resistant[3] without the axiom? The contradiction leads one to make obvious errors[4] in an attempt to rationalize the conflict.

It is common for people to refer cynically to a Bitcoin-like system that omits the resistance axiom as "just another PayPal", a designation not without merit. Confinity[5] originally attempted to create a system with a similar value proposition[6] to Bitcoin. Having failed to do so it discarded the axiom, building the PayPal[7] we know today.

Reference

[1] https://en.wikipedia.org/wiki/Spherical_geometry

[2] Chapter: Permissionless Principle

[3] Chapter: Censorship Resistance Property

[4] Chapter: Hearn Error

[5] https://en.wikipedia.org/wiki/Confinity

[6] Chapter: Value Proposition

[7] https://en.wikipedia.org/wiki/PayPal

Censorship Resistance Property

Resistance to censorship is a consequence of transaction fees. Censorship enforcement is indistinguishable from soft fork enforcement, with majority hash power rejecting non-censoring blocks. Without such enforcement transactions are confirmed on an economically-rational basis despite individual miner subjectivity.

A majority miner is financially profitable. As such there is no cost to acquiring the means of censorship. As mining is necessarily an anonymous[1] role it is always possible for any actor to acquire and deploy majority hash power, and to control it at any given time. As shown in Proof of Work Fallacy[2], hard forks cannot be used to selectively evict the censor and instead accelerate coin collapse.

In the case of active censorship, fees may rise on transactions that fail to confirm. This fee premium creates a greater potential profit for miners who confirm censored transactions. At a sufficient level this opportunity produces additional competition and therefore increasing overall hash rate.

If rising non-censoring hash power exceeds that of the censor, its enforcement fails. The censor is thus faced with the choice of subsidizing operations or abandoning the effort. Only the state can perpetually subsidize operations, as it can compel tax. At the same time it profits from preservation of its own currency regime. **The state must consume taxes to at least the level of the fee premium to maintain censorship enforcement.**

A coin without integrated fees would either fail to a censor or evolve a side fee market. As shown in Side Fee Fallacy[3] it is not necessary that fees be integrated, however fee

Reference

[1] Chapter: Risk Sharing Principle
[2] Chapter: Proof of Work Fallacy
[3] Chapter: Side Fee Fallacy

integration is an important anonymity technique. In either case censorship resistance arises only from the fee premium. The subsidy portion of the block reward does not contribute to censorship resistance because the censor earns the same subsidy as other miners.

It is possible that censorship enforcement could result in a price collapse, causing the censor to incur a loss on operations. However in this case its objective has been achieved, with no opportunity for the economy to counter the censor. This collapse might be achieved at negligible cost by simply demonstrating the intent to censor. It is also possible that a censorship soft fork could lead to a price *increase*, as white market business embraces the associated state approval. Nevertheless, for the coin to survive, its economy must continue to generate a fee premium sufficient to overpower the censor.

It cannot be shown that the economy will generate sufficient fees to overpower a censor. Similarly, it cannot be shown that a censor will be willing and able to subsidize operations at any given level. It is therefore not possible to prove censorship resistance. This is why resistance to state control is axiomatic[1].

Reference

[1] Chapter: Axiom of Resistance

Centralization Risk

Bitcoin weakness[1] results from centralization and from pooling. Forces that produce aggregated mining are called pooling pressures[2]. While pooling weakens confirmation security, centralization weakens the security of consensus rules. Weakness is the result of fewer people with whom to share risk[3].

Consensus risk is shared among active merchants only, as they are the people who have the ability to refuse trade of property for units that fail to conform to their rules. Financial forces that reduce the number of merchants are called centralization pressures. The problem of delegation is that it is commonly coupled with centralization, as is typical in web wallets[4]. The wallet not only owns the saved units but also controls validation of units received in trade. **The latter reduces power over consensus rules to one person for all of the wallets of the service.**

Centralization pressures include:

- Difficulty of use discount.
- On-chain settlement discount.

If exchange is difficult for a customer, the merchant must discount merchandise in order to accept the coin. If exchange is difficult for the merchant, an additional cost is incurred. When referring payments to a trusted third party reduces the size of this discount and/or cost, return on capital is increased.

Reference

[1] Chapter: Qualitative Security Model
[2] Chapter: Pooling Pressure Risk
[3] Chapter: Risk Sharing Principle
[4] https://bitcoin.org/en/wallets/web

Transfer incurs fees which also requires a merchant to discount merchandise. When using a trusted intermediary to settle transfers off-chain reduces fees, and thereby the discount, merchant return on capital is increased.

Centralization manifests as:

- Payment processors
- Web and other trusting wallets
- Hosted APIs for accessing the chain

In a low threat[1] environment the merchant has diminished financial incentive to subsidize Bitcoin security. As the cost of alternatives[2] increases the discount becomes unavoidable. At this point the customer decides to pay a higher price or the merchant closes the business as capital seeks market rates of return.

Reference

[1] Chapter: Threat Level Paradox

[2] https://en.wikipedia.org/wiki/Foreign_exchange_controls

Cockroach Fallacy

There is a theory that aggregation does not materially reduce the security afforded by risk sharing[1] because miners and the economy will disperse as necessary, similar to the scattering cockroaches disturbed by a light. **The theory irrationally implies that security actually exists because it could exist.** This is essentially a rejection of the Threat Level Paradox[2], which implies that security evolves over time under a persistent threat.

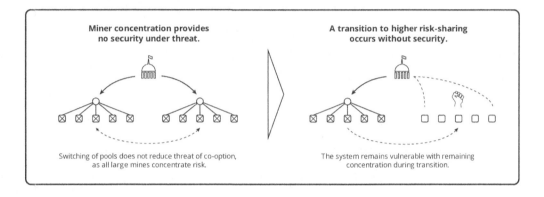

Miner concentration provides no security under threat.

A transition to higher risk-sharing occurs without security.

Switching of pools does not reduce threat of co-option, as all large mines concentrate risk.

The system remains vulnerable with remaining concentration during transition.

The theory relies on grinders switching miner allegiance. This is based on the Balance of Power Fallacy[3], which incorrectly models miners as the threat. A shift of hash power from one mine to another does not reduce pooling or the risk associated[4] with it. The risk is that states co-opt large amounts of hash power, substantially reducing the cost of attack. It is an error to assume that states do not collaborate[5] in defense of seigniorage[6].

Reference

[1] Chapter: Risk Sharing Principle
[2] Chapter: Threat Level Paradox
[3] Chapter: Balance of Power Fallacy
[4] Chapter: Pooling Pressure Risk
[5] http://www.imf.org/external/index.htm
[6] https://en.wikipedia.org/wiki/Seigniorage

> The International Monetary Fund (IMF) is an organization of 189 countries, working to foster global monetary cooperation...
>
> *imf.org*

As such one cannot assume that any large mine can exist outside of state control[1]. A reduction in pooling requires an increase in the number of miners, specifically those who are willing and able to operate covertly[2]. This requires that grinders suffer the increased cost associated with reduced pooling.

Yet people cannot be expected to work against their own financial interest. In order for risk sharing to increase, the financial pressures against it must be reversed. An assumption to the contrary is economically irrational.

The theory also ignores economic centralization and delegation. It is an error to assume the economy can rapidly decentralize, and de-delegation would most likely be infeasible in the case of state attacks as currency controls[3] commonly restrict transfer.

Reference

[1] Chapter: Threat Level Paradox

[2] https://www.theatlantic.com/magazine/archive/2017/09/big-in-venezuela/534177/

[3] https://en.wikipedia.org/wiki/Foreign_exchange_controls

Consensus Property

People generally think of consensus in the context of a fixed membership, like a jury[1]. In this model consensus implies that all members must agree. **But because Bitcoin membership is permissionless and therefore not fixed, there is always complete agreement, as implied by membership.** In this model consensus refers to the size of the membership (economy), not a condition of agreement.

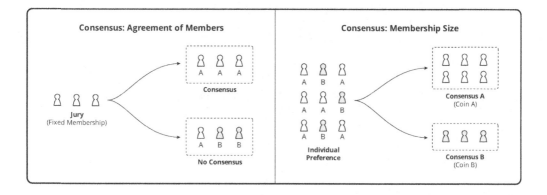

A consensus may fragment[2] or consolidate[3]. Generally a larger consensus provides greater utility and greater security by more broadly sharing risk[4].

Reference

[1] https://en.m.wikipedia.org/wiki/Hung_jury

[2] Chapter: Fragmentation Principle

[3] Chapter: Consolidation Principle

[4] Chapter: Risk Sharing Principle

Cryptodynamic Principles

Cryptodynamics is a term coined here for the purpose of easily referring to the fundamental principles of Bitcoin. This is intended to both inform understanding of Bitcoin and differentiate it from other technologies. The principles are the minimal subset of cryptoeconomic principles necessary to achieve this objective.

While the choice of name is not too important, a rationale for it is provided below.

Crypto[1]

> "A crypto currency is a [money] that uses strong cryptography to secure financial transactions, control the creation of additional units, and verify the transfer of [units]."
>
> *Wikipedia*

Dynamics[2]

> "Dynamics is the branch of applied mathematics [...] concerned with the study of forces [...] and their effect on motion."
>
> *Wikipedia*

Crypto + Dynamics

Cryptodynamics is the set of forces that secure Bitcoin transactions by controlling (1) definition of units, and (2) transfer of units.

Reference

[1] https://en.m.wikipedia.org/wiki/Cryptocurrency

[2] https://en.m.wikipedia.org/wiki/Dynamics_(mechanics)

Principles

Security force is entirely human in nature. People must act to secure anything, including Bitcoin. As an economic system, Bitcoin security can only expect people to act in an economically-rational manner (self-interest). As such Bitcoin security forces are entirely based on the self-interested actions of individual persons, specifically:

- Risk Sharing[1]
- Energy Sinking[2]
- Power Regulating[3]

These forces depend upon each other in order. Without risk sharing energy cannot be sunk into the system to regulate the power of a censor. With these three forces intact Bitcoin can be secure. Without any one of them a technology is not Bitcoin.

It cannot be assumed[4] that, given the incorporation of these forces, a Bitcoin implementation is securable. Furthermore one may be more so than another. **It is only the case that given the incorporation of these forces a technology is a Bitcoin and that without them it is not.**

The possibility of security afforded by these forces can be referred to as "cryptodynamic security". So, for example, a "permissioned blockchain" violates the risk sharing principle, a strictly proof-of-stake technology violates the energy sinking principle, and a money entirely reliant on subsidy for confirmation compensation violates the power regulating principle. None of these are cryptodynamically secure.

Reference

[1] Chapter: Risk Sharing Principle
[2] Chapter: Proof of Stake Fallacy
[3] Chapter: Censorship Resistance Property
[4] Chapter: Axiom of Resistance

Custodial Risk Principle

When a contract represents an asset, the contract is a claim against the asset's custodian. This claim is often called a security, with the intended implication that the claim is "secured" against custodial failure to exchange the asset under the terms of the contract. The monetary value of the security is that of the underlying asset minus the exchange and claim enforcement costs.

Custodial risk is a central aspect of any money[1]. The usefulness of a money is limited by the reliability of its custodian. Being human, the reliability of a custodian cannot be assured. In the case of state money, the single custodian is the state. As shown in Reservation Principle[2] state money exists for the purpose of accumulating a reserve. This provides a benefit to the state only because its custodial role can be abrogated both through liquidation of the reserve and issuance of fraudulent securities. In other words, custodial default is the reason for state money.

The monetary value of a unit of Bitcoin is strictly a function of what it can acquire in trade. If no merchant accepts it, a unit is not useful to its owner. Bitcoin is non-custodial, but in the interest of establishing a general principle, one may consider the set of all merchants the collective Bitcoin custodian. As such the custodial risk is spread across the economy.

In the case of Bitcoin, merchants offer their own property in exchange for the money. As such there is no implied securitization of the property. A merchant can cease to accept any money, which reduces the utility of the money. This can be considered a custodial risk, but not a default as the merchant has accepted no obligation to trade for the money.

Reference

[1] Chapter: Money Taxonomy
[2] Chapter: Reservation Principle

As shown in Fragmentation Principle[1], changing merchant acceptance is the nature of a split.

As shown in Blockchain Fallacy[2], "blockchain technology" can offer no defense against custodial default. A "tokenized" asset is a security. The opportunity for fraud or theft by the custodian, either directly or as compelled by the state, is not reduced. **Just as with commodity monies, such as gold, the custodial risk reduction afforded by Bitcoin is not a consequence of technology or contractual obligation, but the size of its economy.** Ironically it is the "security" that is insecure.

Reference

[1] Chapter: Fragmentation Principle
[2] Chapter: Blockchain Fallacy

Hearn Error

There is a theory that a state cannot ban popular things.

This implies that high transaction throughput allows effective defense against attacks and coercion. This in turn implies that Bitcoin can be secured by accepting the centralizing force of very high transaction throughput.

The theory is invalid, as it is based on empirical observation yet rests on a factual error. **It is evident that states actually prefer to ban popular things.** The following is a short list of commonly-banned popular things:

- Drugs
- Gambling
- Prostitution
- Religion
- Speech
- Assembly
- Trade
- Migration
- Weapons
- Labor
- Books
- Money

This error may arise from failure to accept the Axiom of Resistance[1] while continuing to work in Bitcoin. This is likely to produce cognitive dissonance[2]. The subsequent search for relief may lead one here. However the error eventually becomes undeniable, which may lead to a rage-quit[3].

Reference

[1] Chapter: Axiom of Resistance
[2] https://en.wikipedia.org/wiki/Cognitive_dissonance
[3] https://en.wikipedia.org/wiki/Wikipedia:Rage_quit

Hoarding Fallacy

There is a theory that an increased level of hoarding produces an increased level of security in a coin. This is the similar to the Dumping Fallacy[1] but is not necessarily based on a split.

The presumed security benefit to an elevated level of hoarding stems from the theory that an owner has a say in validation and could act to prevent the economy from accepting what the owners collectively consider invalid money. However owners are not acting unless they trade units for something, and in this case, it is the merchant who enforces consensus rules. **The possibility that owners could act in unison does not increase this zero level of control. The theory is therefore invalid.**

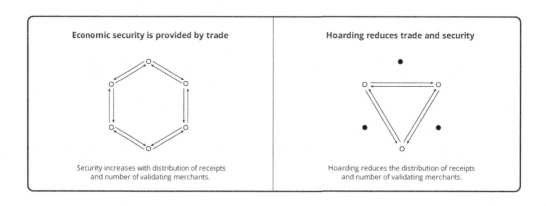

Economic security is provided by trade	Hoarding reduces trade and security
Security increases with distribution of receipts and number of validating merchants.	Hoarding reduces the distribution of receipts and number of validating merchants.

An increase can only be described relative to some base level. If a person can be convinced that there is increased system security in a higher collective hoarding level, the theory holds that the person may decide to hoard more than would otherwise be optimal (i.e. the person's base level). This amounts to an actual individual cost with a presumed

Reference

[1] Chapter: Dumping Fallacy

socialized benefit. In other words the theory depends on irrational economic behavior, even if the security benefit is actual, and is therefore invalid.

The theory implies that less trade in the coin will produce greater security. This is the opposite of the case. As shown in Qualitative Security Model[1], consensus rule enforcement requires ongoing trade. The price of a unit of the coin in another good[2] or money is arbitrary but rises temporarily if individuals are convinced to engage in the fallacy. The benefit of this increase accrues to existing owners. The theory that price can only rise is a related speculative error explored in Lunar Fallacy[3]. Even a provable perpetual general price rise would not validate this theory, as it relates only to a temporary relative increase caused by financially sub-optimal individual decisions.

Reference

[1] Chapter: Qualitative Security Model
[2] Chapter: Inflation Principle
[3] Chapter: Lunar Fallacy

Jurisdictional Arbitrage Fallacy

There is a theory that, since it is unlikely that all states would join a Bitcoin ban, the coin would survive by movement of mining and other activity to permissive states.

Those who do not comply operate in the black market[1] from the perspective of the banning authority. Another state in violation of a ban is considered a rogue state[2] from this perspective. A ban is a simple political action against which Bitcoin offers no protection.

There is a related fallacy[3] that such an action would be impossibly difficult in the case where Bitcoin is popular. This is the idea that Bitcoin is secured by the vote, which reduces its security model to that of the status quo of state money, eliminating Bitcoin's value proposition[4].

White market operations are by definition eliminated by a ban. The theory therefore implies that Bitcoin is ultimately secured by the protection of rogue states. This also reduces to security by vote. Furthermore powerful states have many tools[5] to compel others, everything up to and including open warfare. These tools are commonly employed in various wars, such as those on drugs, money laundering and terror. A Bitcoin ban could easily fall under the umbrella justifications for all of these existing international conflicts.

Reference

[1] https://en.m.wikipedia.org/wiki/Black_market
[2] https://en.m.wikipedia.org/wiki/Rogue_state
[3] Chapter: Hearn Error
[4] Chapter: Value Proposition
[5] https://en.m.wikipedia.org/wiki/United_States_embargoes

However, Bitcoin is specifically designed to operate without permission from any state. Its continued operation as a black market money may lead one or more states to attempt its suppression through censorship[1]. While this may be attempted by a single state, it is common for states to collaborate in defense of the taxing power[2] of their monies. This is the purpose of the International Monetary Fund[3].

Such an action can be executed most efficiently[4] from a single geographical location. In this scenario rogue states offer no defense except to the extent that they are not only willing to forego the tax benefit of their own monies, but also to donate tax money to resist censorship. **It cannot be assumed that rogue states can overpower the censoring authority, and any dependence on them reduces Bitcoin to a politically-secured money.** As such the theory is invalid.

Reference

[1] Chapter: Other Means Principle

[2] https://en.m.wikipedia.org/wiki/Seigniorage

[3] https://www.imf.org

[4] Chapter: Pooling Pressure Risk

Other Means Principle

Bitcoin is an act of resistance[1], an attempt to "gain a new territory of freedom." Freedom contracts through the constant pressure of compulsory financing of the state. It is typical that freedom is expanded through bloodshed, with the specific objective of reducing state power. Bitcoin cannot eliminate the need for personal risk in achieving this objective. However, through risk sharing[2] it can potentially reduce the inflation tax[3] without spilling blood. This will not eliminate tax generally; however it may reduce state power by making tax significantly more visible.

This conflict between state and individuals for control of money[4] will pass through up to four phases anticipated by the Bitcoin security model[5]. These may overlap and vary regionally but are each clearly identifiable.

1. Honeymoon
2. Black Market
3. Competition
4. Surrender

Reference

[1] Chapter: Axiom of Resistance

[2] Chapter: Risk Sharing Principle

[3] https://en.wikipedia.org/wiki/Seigniorage

[4] Chapter: Money Taxonomy

[5] Chapter: Qualitative Security Model

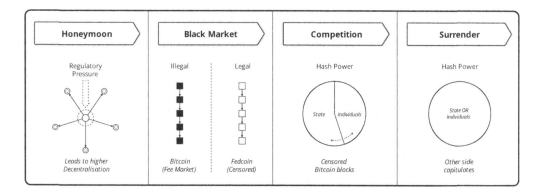

The honeymoon phase is characterized by a desire of state agencies to retain regulatory control over the movement of money and securities. To this end pressure is applied at points of aggregation. As pressure on pooled miners and centralized merchants increases, cost rises and utility drops. The money then necessarily becomes more distributed to avoid these expenses.

As it becomes apparent that controls on points of aggregation are insufficient enforcement, and the awareness surfaces that seigniorage[1] is at risk, transaction and complementary mining of Bitcoin is outlawed[2]. As states collaborate to protect their monies, this may become a global "War on Bitcoin". This may coincide with adoption of an official new money, i.e. Fedcoin[3]. The objective would be to appear to embrace a "safer" money than Bitcoin while retaining the seigniorage and surveillance advantages of electronic state money substitutes.

Assuming sufficient resistance, Bitcoin persists independent of Fedcoin as a black market money. At this point the state concludes that the only effective tactic is to

Reference

[1] https://en.wikipedia.org/wiki/Seigniorage
[2] Chapter: Hearn Error
[3] Chapter: Fedcoin Objectives

compete as a miner. Given that mining is necessarily anonymous[1], there is no way[2] for the economy to prevent state participation in mining. Thus Bitcoin enters the competitive phase[3], with the state attempting a perpetual 51% attack.

Apart from ongoing black market phase enforcement, the competitive phase is characterized by a peaceful hash power battle between the state and individuals. The state operates at a loss due to the rejection of censored transactions. This loss is offset by tax revenue. Fee pressure on censored transactions rises[4] until the state mining tax subsidy is offset by this fee level. **At this point taxes and censored transaction fees both rise until one side of the conflict surrenders.**

In this manner Bitcoin can potentially win a war by other means[5]. It cannot be assumed that this surrender will be perpetual. As implied by the Threat Level Paradox[6], the money is likely to drift into previous phases as the threat diminishes.

Reference

[1] Chapter: Public Data Principle

[2] Chapter: Proof of Work Fallacy

[3] Chapter: Other Means Principle

[4] Chapter: Censorship Resistance Property

[5] https://en.wikiquote.org/wiki/Carl_von_Clausewitz

[6] Chapter: Threat Level Paradox

Patent Resistance Principle

Unlike copyright, patent is an anti-market force. A true copyright is a contractual agreement between buyer and seller, where patent is exclusively a state grant of monopoly[1]. The patent is not an "attack" by the patent-holder, it is a distortion pooling pressure[2] created by the state.

The process of mining is highly competitive. Monopoly protection in the use of efficient mining algorithms[3] is a strong anti-market pooling pressure. Bitcoin is secured by people resisting[4] anti-market forces. Resistance incurs greater risk[5] when the miner is highly pooled and/or non-anonymous[6].

If people do not resist such forces, there is no security[7] in the money. As the threat level[8] increases the consequence of patent violation becomes no more of a risk than mining itself. **As such the impact of patents is inconsequential as it pertains to the security of the money.**

Reference

[1] https://mises.org/library/man-economy-and-state-power-and-market/html/p/1075
[2] Chapter: Pooling Pressure Risk
[3] https://www.asicboost.com/patent
[4] Chapter: Axiom of Resistance
[5] Chapter: Risk Sharing Principle
[6] Chapter: Public Data Principle
[7] Chapter: Qualitative Security Model
[8] Chapter: Threat Level Paradox

Permissionless Principle

Bitcoin is designed[1] to operate without permission from any authority. Its value proposition[2] is entirely based on this property.

A market can be divided into permissioned and permissionless from the perspective of the state. For ease of reference the former is often referred to as "white market" and the latter "black market". White market trade, by definition, requires permission, and black market does not.

As a simple matter of definition, **Bitcoin operations cannot be both white market and permissionless.** Any person operating in the white market requires permission to do so. Bitcoin is therefore inherently a black market money. Its security architecture necessarily assumes it is operating without state permission[3].

The security of Bitcoin does not extend to white market systems. Any system dependent upon the value proposition of Bitcoin must also be black market.

Reference

[1] Chapter: Cryptodynamic Principles

[2] Chapter: Value Proposition

[3] Chapter: Other Means Principle

Prisoner's Dilemma Fallacy

There is a theory that in a choice to join a ban on Bitcoin, individual states face a prisoner's dilemma[1]. A meaningful ban implies one or more states (the "prison") will enforce economic sanctions[2] (at least) on other states (the "prisoners") potentially moving to Bitcoin as a reserve currency[3].

We assume that the prisoners who may decide to use Bitcoin are trading partners. In other words its use as a reserve currency requires a partner with whom to transact.

Ordinal utility[4] is implied by subjective value[5]. No outcome ties[6] are observed, implying strong dilemma. Both symmetric and asymmetric knowledge assumptions are evaluated.

The outcome for individual Bitcoin (Sucker) :

- Economic sanction.

- No trading partners (using Dollar).

- An unusable reserve currency (no trading partners).

The outcome for mutual Bitcoin (Reward) :

- Economic sanction.

- Economic sanction of trading partner.

Reference

[1] https://en.wikipedia.org/wiki/Prisoner%27s_dilemma
[2] https://www.cfr.org/backgrounder/what-are-economic-sanctions
[3] https://en.wikipedia.org/wiki/Reserve_currency
[4] https://en.wikipedia.org/wiki/Ordinal_utility
[5] https://en.wikipedia.org/wiki/Subjective_theory_of_value
[6] https://en.wikipedia.org/wiki/Tie_(draw)

- A reserve currency not taxed via seigniorage.

The outcome for individual Dollar (Temptation):

- No economic sanction.
- Economic sanction of trading partner.
- A reserve currency taxed via seigniorage.

The outcome for mutual Dollar (Punishment):

- No economic sanction.
- No economic sanction of trading partner.
- A reserve currency taxed via seigniorage.

Strong Symmetric Dilemma With Ordinal Outcome Relations

Brazil\Ireland	Bitcoin	Dollar
Bitcoin	R\R	S\T
Dollar	T\S	P\P

To be considered a prisoner's dilemma T > R > P > S must be true where:

- T > R and P > S imply that Dollar is the dominant strategy for each.
- R > P implies that mutual Bitcoin is preferred by each to mutual Dollar.

We can conclude that P > S holds, as individual sanction implies no international settlement and therefore no benefit from a foreign exchange reserve[1], and presumably sanctions are undesirable.

To determine if R > P and T > R hold, an objective method is required to relate only seigniorage and sanction, as presumably sanctions are undesirable. This can be obtained by the observation that Gold is subject to neither seigniorage[2] nor sanction. In other words Gold provides the above benefits of Bitcoin without sanction. Yet Gold has not been chosen (and was previously dropped in favor of Dollar), which implies the Dollar outcome is preferred to Gold and therefore Bitcoin. As such, neither of the dominant strategies[3] hold. **As such there is no dilemma.**

Strong Asymmetric Dilemma With Ordinal Outcome Relations

Brazil\Ireland	Bitcoin	Dollar
Bitcoin	Rr\Rc	Sr\Tc
Dollar	Tr\Sc	Pr\Pc

To be considered a prisoner's dilemma Ti > Ri > Pi > Si must be true where:

- Tr > Rr and Pr > Sr

- Tc > Rc and Pc > Sc

- Rr > Pr and Rc > Pc

Reference

[1] https://en.wikipedia.org/wiki/Foreign-exchange_reserves
[2] https://en.wikipedia.org/wiki/Seigniorage
[3] https://en.wikipedia.org/wiki/Strategic_dominance

If these relations all hold then individual Dollar is preferred to Bitcoin, and mutual Bitcoin is preferred. Given that these are the same relations evaluated in the symmetric scenario, there is no dilemma.

Other Assumptions

The Gold-Bitcoin relation assumes that clearing[1] costs, of transporting Gold and confirming Bitcoin, are negligible[2] in the context of international settlement. Clearing requires periodic movement of only payment imbalances between states.

> ... any correction of an economic imbalance would be accelerated and normally it would not be necessary to wait for the point at which substantial quantities of gold needed to be transported from one country to another.
>
> *gold.org*

Dollar has been preferred to Gold despite having similar weight, significantly larger size, and seigniorage. The Gold-Bitcoin relation assumes no distinction in volatility and liquidity, though Gold objectively outperforms[3] Bitcoin in both areas. Given that Gold and Bitcoin are both stable monies[4], no speculative return is assumed for either. Other Gold, Bitcoin and Dollar monetary properties are assumed to be either equivalent or not relevant to state reserve currency.

Reference

[1] https://en.wikipedia.org/wiki/Clearing_(finance)

[2] https://www.gold.org/about-gold/history-of-gold/the-gold-standard

[3] https://coinweek.com/bullion-report/bitcoin-vs-gold-10-crystal-clear-comparisons

[4] Chapter: Stability Property

Private Key Fallacy

Private keys do not secure Bitcoin, they secure units of Bitcoin. **Private key control applies to individual security, not system security.** Whoever controls keys is the owner, and Bitcoin provides security for that owner, even if the keys are stolen. Decentralized validation secures consensus and distributed majority hash power secures confirmation, but private key security is the owner's problem.

Proof of Work Fallacy

Merchants purchase mining services that meet their rules for a satisfactory fee. There is a theory that mining services are subservient in this trade. This subservience is sometimes described as "asymmetry" or "users rule". This theory leads people to believe that mining can be strongly pooled as long as merchants are not centralized, as the economy can control the behavior of mining, rendering the system secure. The consequence of this invalid theory is complacency regarding the insecurity caused by pooling.

Miners control transaction selection, while merchants control property offered in exchange. If some part of the economy is unsatisfied with the selections of miners, it can offer its property for sale in a split coin with a different work rule that obsoletes all grinding hardware. This is typically described as a proof-of-work hard fork.

According to this theory miners then suffer a catastrophic loss due to the unrecoverable capital investment in highly-specialized hardware. The hard fork may include a difficulty adjustment, allowing confirmation to continue despite a presumed significant drop in hash rate. Due to the lower difficulty and a presumed lack of specialized hardware, more individuals are able to mine. This introduces new miners to the business and reduces pooling.

It has been said that this ability of the economy to foist a capital loss on its trading partners is an asymmetry unique in comparison to other markets. For example, an apple buying community cannot simply "destroy" the orchards of all of its suppliers. **The theory fails to recognize that there is no asymmetry in trade.** If all apple buyers decide that they will buy no apples from existing orchards they certainly have that power.

Similarly, the orchards have the option to not sell. Price is the continual resolution of this tension. This is exactly the same dynamic that exists in every market.

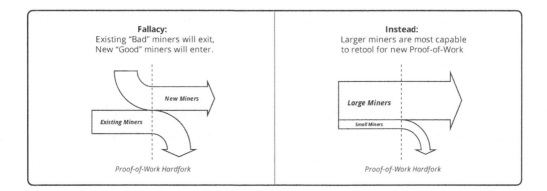

The theory also fails to account for lack of identity. It assumes that the capital loss will cause the exit of existing "bad" miners and the entry of new "good" miners. This is an unsupportable assumption. There is no reason to believe that existing miners will exit nor is there any reason to believe that new miners would not make the same decisions as previous miners given that they are in the same business, assuming one could even tell the difference. At least in the apple scenario one knows from whom one is buying apples and can discriminate, this is not possible in Bitcoin.

The theory also fails to account for the economics of mining. There is an advantage to proximity[1] that produces greater returns on capital for miners with greater hash power. Larger miners are therefore more profitable than small miners. Larger miners will therefore be better capitalized than their smaller competition. When the rule change occurs the miners that remain will be those who can afford to retool, which will be the largest.

It is irrational to assume that all miners will simply exit. Would we expect all apple growers to be replaced by new apple growers? In mining are not expertise, facilities, energy contracts, process, and non-specialized machinery important advantages over newcomers? Existing miners have an inherent advantage over their supposed

Reference

[1] Chapter: Proximity Premium Flaw

replacements. This means they have greater access to capital. So not only do larger miners end up with less competition, all existing miners that remain have an advantage over any new miners.

The theory also fails to consider that merchants need mining. Mining is not replaced by splitting, and it retains complete control over transaction selection. So for example if the "bad" miners happen to be states that are attacking the coin, the state itself and co-opted miners will continue with the same disruption, at a lower energy cost. As other miners fail due to what is effectively a 100% tax, the attacker's energy cost continues to decrease. Mining services that are "good" for merchants cannot be produced by splitting.

Finally, the theory fails to recognize insurance consequences. Based on the previous capital loss experienced by all miners for a given coin, all future miners of its replacement will insure against the likelihood of a similar event. They may self-insure, but the increased cost is unavoidable. This will reduce hash rate for the same fee until the possibility of such an event is deemed negligible. So the economy reduces its own double-spend security and ends up with the same miners and greater pooling. This is a reduction of security on two levels, with no benefit.

Public Data Principle

It follows from the Risk Sharing Principle[1] that system security depends upon covert mining and trade. A coin exists as a mutually-beneficial[2] market between miners and merchants for the confirmation of transactions within blocks in exchange for fees.

The necessarily covert activities are listed by role:

Miner

- obtain blocks [to build upon]
- obtain unconfirmed transactions [to earn fees from]
- create and distribute blocks [to cause others to build upon]
- receive payment for confirmations [to finance operations]

Merchant

- obtain blocks [to validate customer payment]
- obtain unconfirmed transactions (optional) [to anticipate payments and fees]
- create and distribute transactions [to obtain customer payment]
- make payment for confirmations [to compensate confirmation]

If blocks cannot be obtained anonymously the system is insecure. The inability to obtain the strongest blocks available to other people is a network partition, which implies localized insecurity. However neither anonymity, nor its opposite identity, can ensure one sees the strongest branch at any given time. In other words, any attempt to mitigate

Reference

[1] Chapter: Risk Sharing Principle
[2] Chapter: Balance of Power Fallacy

partitioning with the introduction of identity is a false choice[1] that sacrifices system security for the false promise of ensuring localized security.

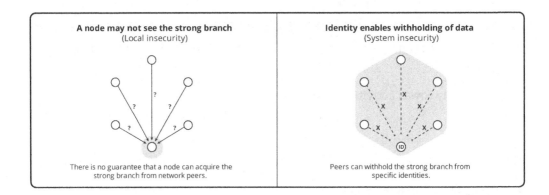

A node may not see the strong branch (Local insecurity)	Identity enables withholding of data (System insecurity)
There is no guarantee that a node can acquire the strong branch from network peers.	Peers can withhold the strong branch from specific identities.

It is not essential that all miners or merchants see all transactions at any given time. However broad visibility is preferable as it produces the most robust competition for fees and best leading information. In

other words, a market where every participant sees all of the transactions all of the time is a perfect market[2]. Asking the network for specific transactions, as opposed to all (or summary information about all), is a source of taint and must be avoided in the interest of security as well.

Creation of blocks and transactions does not inherently expose identity, however public distribution of either is the primary source of taint. To the extent that miners openly self-identify, they are relying on the assumption of a low-threat environment[3], not contributing to system security. Avoiding taint when disseminating blocks and

Reference

[1] https://en.wikipedia.org/wiki/False_dilemma

[2] https://en.wikipedia.org/wiki/Perfect_competition

[3] Chapter: Threat Level Paradox

transactions requires use of an anonymous connection[1] to a community server. This ensures the distribution network never has access to identifying information.

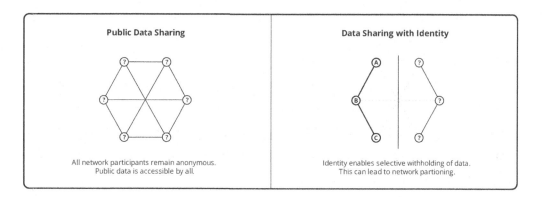

Public Data Sharing	Data Sharing with Identity
All network participants remain anonymous. Public data is accessible by all.	Identity enables selective withholding of data. This can lead to network partioning.

Proof-of-work preserves the anonymity of miners. There is no signature associated with mining and energy is presumed to be ubiquitous. Similarly, the ability to pay anonymously for confirmation is the reason for transaction fee inclusion. It is sufficient[2] to pay a miner directly (off chain) for confirmation, however this exposes the merchant and miner to each other, and makes it more difficult to estimate fees anonymously.

Bitcoin is novel in that all financial transactions can be validated from public data and without identity. Centralized financial systems rely on either trust in (cryptographically-identifiable) connections to other parties or trust in (cryptographically-verifiable) signatures on transmitted data. This is the essence of trust-based systems; certain authorities have secrets that others use to verify that authenticity. **The reason for validation is to eliminate the use of identity and thereby authority.**

Reference

[1] https://en.wikipedia.org/wiki/Anonymizer

[2] Chapter: Side Fee Fallacy

Qualitative Security Model

Decentralization Model

In Social Network Principle[1] it is shown that Bitcoin is a network of human relationships. This can be modelled as a directed graph[2] where each vertex represents a merchant and each edge represents a trade for bitcoin. Edges indicate the direction of movement of coin and are quantified in the number of units traded. All owners are presumed to have been merchants at the time of coin receipt, including as miners (selling confirmations) and as recipients of charity (selling goodwill[3]).

If a person is not personally accepting coin, or does not personally validate coin accepted, the person cannot reject invalid coin. The person is entrusting this task to a central authority. **All people utilizing the same delegate are reduced to just one vertex that represents the delegate.**

For any period of time, economic security is a function of the number of merchants and the similarity of amounts traded. The strongest economy would be all people in the world trading for the same number of units in the period, an ideal which can be called a "distributed" (or fully-decentralized) economy. The weakest would be one delegate accepting all units traded in the period, which would be a "centralized" economy.

More specifically, the system is most economically decentralized which has the greatest number of vertices (merchants) with the lowest coefficient of variation[4] in the incoming

Reference

[1] Chapter: Social Network Principle

[2] https://en.wikipedia.org/wiki/Graph_(discrete_mathematics)#Directed_graph

[3] https://en.wikipedia.org/wiki/Goodwill_(accounting)

[4] https://en.wikipedia.org/wiki/Coefficient_of_variation

edges (receipts). Defining a distribution function as the inverse of coefficient of variation we obtain:

```
economic-decentralization = distribution(receipts) * merchants
```

Similar to economic security, confirmation security can be modelled as an edgeless graph[1]. Each miner is represented by one vertex on the graph. A grinder is not a miner as the grinder has no decision-making ability, only the miner is represented. The total hash power employed by a miner is the weight of the vertex.

For any period of time, confirmation security is a function of the number of miners and the similarity of hash power they directed. The strongest censorship resistance would be all people in the world mining at the same hash power in the period, an ideal which can be called "distributed" (or fully-decentralized) confirmation. The weakest would be one miner with 100% of hash power, which would be "centralized" confirmation.

More specifically, the system is most decentralized in confirmation which has the greatest number of vertices (miners) with the highest distribution in weights (hash power):

```
confirmation-decentralization = distribution(hash-power) * miners
```

Security Model

Decentralization alone is not security. Security is the product of activity, distribution of that activity, and the fraction of participating humanity.

Reference

[1] https://en.wikipedia.org/wiki/Null_graph

```
security = activity * distribution * participation
```

Given that there is no limit to humanity, trade or computation, the level of security in each axis is unbounded. Security is also unbounded with perfect distribution (i.e. infinite decentralization). A minimum level of zero in each is achieved with either no participation or no activity. Economic and confirmation security can thus be defined as:

```
economic-security = receipts * distribution(receipts) * [merchants /
humanity]

confirmation-security = hash-power * distribution(hash-power) * [miners /
humanity]
```

Limits of the Model

These relations do not say anything about the absolute effectiveness represented by any value, or the relative effectiveness of any two values except that a greater value represents a greater effectiveness. This is not due to a deficiency in the model. The factors include people, specifically the effectiveness of their individual abilities to resist[1] and their perception of value in the money. All who validate or mine offer some level of resistance, but there is no implied continuity. We refer to a "level" of security, not an "amount" of security.

As show in Public Data Principle[2], anonymity is a tool that aids in defending one's ability to trade and/or mine. As such the level of decentralization can never be measured; the model is a conceptual aid. As shown in Balance of Power Fallacy[3], the security afforded by each of the two sub-models is complementary and independent of the other. While

Reference

[1] Chapter: Axiom of Resistance
[2] Chapter: Public Data Principle
[3] Chapter: Balance of Power Fallacy

people could decide to trade and/or mine independently in the future, the Cockroach Fallacy[1] shows that they are not contributing to security until they do so. The model represents security as it exists in the period.

Reference

[1] Chapter: Cockroach Fallacy

Risk Sharing Principle

Bitcoin is not secured by blockchains[1], hash power, validation, decentralization, cryptography[2], open source[3] or game theory[4] – it is secured by people.

Technology is never the root of system security. Technology is a tool to help people secure what they value. Security requires people to act. A server cannot be secured by a firewall if there is no lock on the door to the server room, and a lock cannot secure the server room without a guard to monitor the door, and a guard cannot secure the door without risk of personal harm.

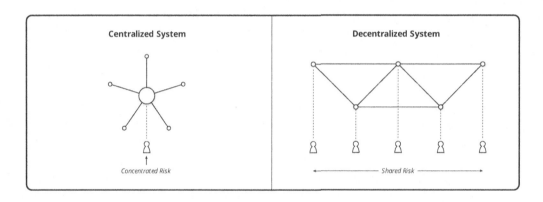

Bitcoin is no different, it is secured by people who place themselves at personal risk. Sharing this risk with other people is the purpose of decentralization. A centralized system[5] requires one person[6] to shoulder all of its risk. A decentralized system divides

Reference

[1] https://en.wikipedia.org/wiki/Blockchain
[2] https://en.wikipedia.org/wiki/Cryptography
[3] https://en.wikipedia.org/wiki/Free_and_open-source_software
[4] Chapter: Prisoner's Dilemma Fallacy
[5] https://en.wikipedia.org/wiki/Liberty_Reserve
[6] https://en.wikipedia.org/wiki/Ross_Ulbricht

risk among individuals[1] who comprise system security. Those who do not understand the value of decentralization most likely do not understand the necessary role[2] of people in security.

Bitcoin allows people to share the personal risk of accepting and mining coin. It is only the willingness and ability of these people to resist[3] that can prevent coercion of their nodes and co-option of their mines, and this is what actually secures Bitcoin. If people do not accept these risks, there is no effective security in the money. If a great many people do so individual risk is minimized. Bitcoin is a tool, not magic.

Reference

[1] https://en.wikipedia.org/wiki/BitTorrent
[2] https://www.theatlantic.com/magazine/archive/2017/09/big-in-venezuela/534177
[3] Chapter: Axiom of Resistance

Social Network Principle

In the terminology of Paul Baran's 1964 paper on distributed networks[1] the importance of topology in network design is the ability of communications to withstand the loss of a certain number of nodes. A centralized (star) network will fail with the loss of one node. A distributed (mesh) network is more resilient. A hybrid of these systems is considered decentralized.

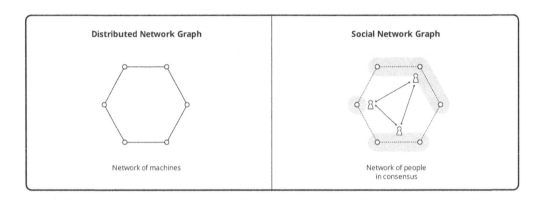

As a money Bitcoin forms a social graph. Only a person can decide to accept one money[2] or another in trade. A set of people sharing the same definition for a money is referred to as a consensus. Authority in a monetary system is the power to define the money. Bitcoin is a tool that people can use to defend against the tendency toward authority, in order to preserve their agreement and therefore utility in the money.

In distributed systems terminology a Bitcoin "node" is a person and the system is money. It does not matter how many machines the person controls, the loss of that person is a loss of a node in the system (including all of the person's machines).

Reference

[1] http://web.cs.ucla.edu/classes/cs217/Baran64.pdf

[2] Chapter: Money Taxonomy

A centralized money cannot withstand the loss of one person. If that one person changes their rules, the original money ceases to exist. As shown in Risk Sharing Principle[1], Bitcoin relies on decentralization to allow people to resist[2] authority. This decentralization makes the money more able to withstand the loss of more people when faced with state attacks. A loss in this sense is the refusal of the person to trade in the money.

Reference

[1] Chapter: Risk Sharing Principle

[2] Chapter: Axiom of Resistance

Threat Level Paradox

As implied by the Zero Sum Property[1], presumably the only way to defeat external subsidy[2] is to mine at a capital loss relative to market return on capital. Similarly it seems that only way to defeat tax, up to and including a 100% tax (prohibition), is to mine beyond the reach of the taxing authority, such as in secret. As with all black markets[3] there is an increased cost to subversive mining[4]. Competing against subsidized mining compounds the cost.

If one accepts the Axiom of Resistance[5] one must assume that both tax and subsidy will be used to reduce the cost of controlling Bitcoin. Using the power to subsidize mining (via tax revenues), states can cause pooling in the region of the subsidy. Once majority hash power is focused the state can use its taxing (regulatory) power in the region to compel censorship.

Therefore in order to enjoy the benefits of a Bitcoin, it would seem that people will ultimately have to mine at a loss. However, censorship creates the opportunity for others to mine profitably to the extent that people are willing to offset this cost with fees. This black market is Bitcoin's censorship resistance.

Reference

[1] Chapter: Zero Sum Property

[2] https://en.wikipedia.org/wiki/Subsidy

[3] https://en.wikipedia.org/wiki/Black_market

[4] https://www.theatlantic.com/magazine/archive/2017/09/big-in-venezuela/534177

[5] Chapter: Axiom of Resistance

Bitcoin in a low threat environment:

Bitcoin in a high threat environment:

Pooling pressures are financially advantageous for individuals.

Efficiency gains of pooling are outweighed by the cost of an larger attack surface.

People pay a higher price for certain transactions, and in order to maintain that higher price the state must also suffer the expense, despite its ineffectiveness.

Paradoxically, this tool works well when money is under attack and poorly otherwise. If there was no *internal* pooling-pressure[1] these cases would be balanced. But risk distribution[2] is essential to subversive mining, and pooling pressure works *against* distribution. So there is ever-expanding attack surface[3] with no pressure to contract unless effective monetary alternatives are suppressed. The suppression[4] of alternatives raises reward utility to the miner in the region of suppression. The paradox applies as well to centralization pressures[5].

The expected consequence is that Bitcoin will not be well prepared for attacks because it is financially disadvantageous for people in a low threat environment.

Reference

[1] Chapter: Pooling Pressure Risk
[2] Chapter: Risk Sharing Principle
[3] https://en.wikipedia.org/wiki/Attack_surface
[4] https://en.wikipedia.org/wiki/Foreign_exchange_controls
[5] Chapter: Centralization Risk

Value Proposition

The value of Bitcoin over its alternatives derives directly from removing the state from control over both monetary supply and transaction censorship. Advantages include freedom from seigniorage[1], foreign exchange controls[2], and financial surveillance[3]. These allow the money to be transferred to any person, in any place, at any time, without need for third party permission.

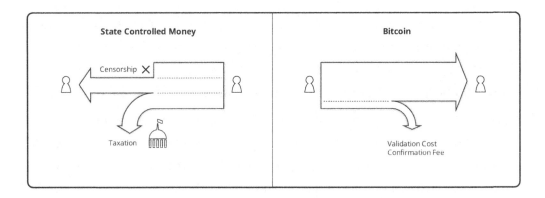

These advantages represent cost reduction through the avoidance of tax. Seigniorage is directly a tax, while foreign exchange controls limit its evasion. The state itself often claims political independence[4] as an objective in the interest of limiting this taxing power. Financial surveillance limits tax evasion more generally. **While Bitcoin cannot eliminate tax, or even necessarily reduce total takings, it represents a change in the nature of taxation.** In any case, for those who consider the state a social good, the option to voluntarily fund it remains.

Reference

[1] https://en.m.wikipedia.org/wiki/Seigniorage

[2] https://en.m.wikipedia.org/wiki/Foreign_exchange_controls

[3] https://en.m.wikipedia.org/wiki/Know_your_customer

[4] https://www.federalreserve.gov/faqs/about_12799.htm

It would be an error to assume these advantages flow from the existence of a more efficient technology than employed by monopoly monies[1]. The technology is far less efficient[2], yet it helps people[3] resist state controls. It is this resistance[4] that provides the value.

Reference

[1] Chapter: Money Taxonomy

[2] Chapter: Scalability Principle

[3] Chapter: Risk Sharing Principle

[4] Chapter: Axiom of Resistance

STATISM

Fedcoin Objectives

As implied by Value Proposition[1] there are two aspects of Bitcoin that make it a target of state controls, both threats to tax revenue.

In combating[2] Bitcoin the state may attempt to introduce a cosmetically similar money[3], which can be referred to as Fedcoin. This could be introduced as a split or alternative coin. The objective would be to preserve the superficial aspects of Bitcoin while eliminating its value proposition. This would protect tax revenues while allowing proponents to propagandize Fedcoin as a "safer" alternative to Bitcoin. Fedcoin is not itself relevant to Bitcoin except to the extent that the act of compelling its use requires resistance[4].

The essential Fedcoin distinctions from Bitcoin allow the state to arbitrarily create new units (seigniorage[5]) and deny transfer (censorship). The seigniorage objective can be achieved by a hard fork that introduces one new consensus rule. This rule allows the introduction of new units in the case where the state has signed an inflationary transaction. The censorship objective can be achieved by a soft fork that precludes confirmation of transactions that lack state signature.

Preventing the state from compelling the use of these forks is the central purpose of Bitcoin system security. The economy guards against the hard fork and miners guard against the soft fork. The risks[6] taken by these people preserve the value of the money relative to state-controlled alternatives.

Reference

[1] Chapter: Value Proposition
[2] Chapter: Other Means Principle
[3] Chapter: Money Taxonomy
[4] Chapter: Axiom of Resistance
[5] https://en.m.wikipedia.org/wiki/Seigniorage
[6] Chapter: Risk Sharing Principle

Inflationary Quality Fallacy

There is a theory that the price inflation[1] caused by seigniorage[2] causes the production of lower "quality" and/or less durable[3] goods. Durability is one of many qualities that a person might value in one good over another. **The theory necessarily presumes that value is objective and therefore contradicts the subjective theory of value.** As such the theory is invalid.

There is no provable relation between the number of units of money[4] required to trade for a good and the qualities of a good that one might prefer. Greater wealth (which is perception, as value is subjective[5]), implies lower time preference[6], as implied by the theory of marginal utility[7]. However even under the assumption of a misperception of increasing wealth, lower time preference does not imply a preference for lower "quality" goods. It implies only an increasing willingness to lend a greater portion of one's capital. Rothbard[8] makes this "subtle" error in *What Has Government Done to Our Money*[9], one that continues to be perpetuated.

> The quality of work will decline in an inflation for a more subtle reason: people become enamored of "get-rich-quick" schemes, seemingly within their grasp in an era of ever-rising prices, and often scorn sober effort.
>
> *Murray Rothbard: What has Government Done to Our Money*

Reference

[1] https://en.m.wikipedia.org/wiki/Inflation

[2] https://en.m.wikipedia.org/wiki/Seigniorage

[3] Chapter: Depreciation Principle

[4] Chapter: Money Taxonomy

[5] https://en.m.wikipedia.org/wiki/Subjective_theory_of_value

[6] Chapter: Time Preference Fallacy

[7] https://en.m.wikipedia.org/wiki/Marginal_utility

[8] https://en.m.wikipedia.org/wiki/Murray_Rothbard

[9] https://mises.org/library/what-has-government-done-our-money/html/p/81

It is assumed, certainly by Rothbard, that people *always* prefer to get rich sooner than later, as implied by the axiom of time preference. And as shown by the Fisher Hypothesis[1], to the extent that price inflation is predictable it is offset in the real interest rate[2]. To the extent it is not predictable Rothbard's conjecture does not apply.

Seigniorage is a tax, which makes people poorer. Being poorer *increases* time preference, the opposite effect described by the theory. All tax shifts property involuntarily from some people to other people, as that is its only actual mechanism and objective respectively. As Rothbard himself elaborates in his significantly more rigorous *Man Economy and State*[3], the form of the tax is economically irrelevant.

> For all these reasons, the goal of uniformity of taxation is an impossible one. It is not simply difficult to achieve in practice; it is conceptually impossible and self-contradictory.
>
> *Murray Rothbard: Man Economy and State*

Therefore it cannot even be shown that seigniorage itself makes those taxed poorer than the taxes it presumably replaces. Only a net increase in tax implies a reduction in wealth.

Reference

[1] https://en.m.wikipedia.org/wiki/Fisher_hypothesis

[2] https://en.m.wikipedia.org/wiki/Real_interest_rate

[3] https://mises.org/library/man-economy-and-state-power-and-market/html/ppp/1393

Reservation Principle

The term "reserve"[1] refers to a hoard of capital, as distinct from that portion of savings which is invested. Both states and people hoard capital to satisfy expected liquidity requirements. The term "reserve currency"[2] refers to a state hoard, as required for settlement[3] of accounts with other states. Money reserves of people within a state generally consist of the state's issued money – primarily notes or fiat, with a lesser amount in coin[4].

States buy reserve currency from people using monopoly money[5], foreign exchange controls[6] and direct taxation. Using their own money discounts purchases by the amount of seigniorage[7]. Foreign exchange controls restrict or prohibit use of the reserve currency as money. By treating the reserve currency as property but not money, the state creates a tax on the apparent capital gain[8] in the reserve money when it devalues its money[9] against the reserve money through monetary inflation[10]. Official exchange rates[11] below market value create another tax on use of the reserve currency.

A "gold standard" is one in which the state collects gold as a foreign exchange reserve, and individuals reserve in claims to a "standard" amount. The U.S. Dollar was

Reference

[1] Chapter: Reserve Definition

[2] https://en.wikipedia.org/wiki/Reserve_currency

[3] https://en.wikipedia.org/wiki/Settlement_(finance)

[4] https://en.wikipedia.org/wiki/Commodity_money

[5] Chapter: Money Taxonomy

[6] https://en.wikipedia.org/wiki/Foreign_exchange_controls

[7] https://en.wikipedia.org/wiki/Seigniorage

[8] https://www.investopedia.com/articles/personal-finance/081616/understanding-taxes-physical-goldsilver-investments.asp

[9] https://en.wikipedia.org/wiki/Inflation

[10] https://en.wikipedia.org/wiki/Monetary_inflation

[11] https://en.wikipedia.org/wiki/Exchange_rate#Parallel_exchange_rate

established[1] as redeemable in gold at $20.67 per ounce in 1834. For 100 years the state bought and sold gold at this rate. In 1934 the Dollar was devalued[2] by 60%, to $35 per ounce. At this point its redeemability (by people) was abrogated, and it was made unlawful for them to hoard or contract in it. This irredeemably was extended[3] to other states in 1971, officially ending the gold standard in the United States. No longer a debt of the state, the Dollar transitioned from a representative currency[4] (i.e. note) to fiat.

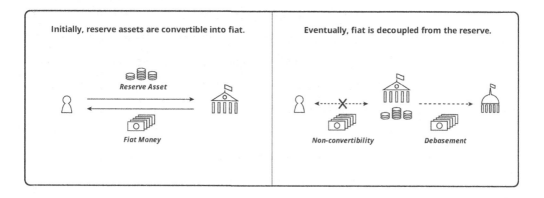

The U.S. primary foreign exchange reserve is gold[5] (74.5%) with the remainder in foreign currency and equivalents, whereas citizens primarily reserve using the Dollar. A state's own notes or fiat are not generally usable as its own foreign exchange reserve, as the state can abrogate or devalue its payment.

Reference

[1] https://en.wikipedia.org/wiki/Coinage_Act_of_1834
[2] https://en.wikipedia.org/wiki/Gold_Reserve_Act
[3] https://en.wikipedia.org/wiki/Nixon_shock
[4] https://en.wikipedia.org/wiki/Representative_money
[5] https://en.wikipedia.org/wiki/Gold_reserve

The U.S. Treasury reports that it hoards[1] over 8,000 metric tons of gold, worth approximately $400,000,000,000. The purchasing power of the U.S. Dollar note in 1834 was about 30 times that of U.S. Dollar fiat in 2019.

The purpose of a reserve currency is to tax. The state first buys the reserve money with negotiable promissory notes[2], then issues more notes than it has money in reserve, then abrogates the notes and retains the reserve. The devaluation of the notes is the result of excess issuance (seigniorage) and is a tax on those who hoard them. The state collects the reserve money into its hoard, which represents its ability to settle its own debts with other states. While people do still hoard the reserve money, it is subject to onerous constraints[3] on its use in order to preserve the tax benefit of the state's monopoly money. These constraints tighten as the level of the tax rises.

The use of gold as a state reserve offers no monetary benefit to individuals who must still trade in monopoly money. As shown in Reserve Currency Fallacy[4], Bitcoin as a state reserve can do no better. However, unlike gold, Bitcoin's definition is in the hands of those who accept it in trade. With the bulk of actual bitcoin acceptance in the hands of the state, with people trading in money substitutes[5], there is nothing to restrain the state from introducing both arbitrary inflation and censorship.

Reference

[1] https://www.treasury.gov/resource-center/data-chart-center/IR-Position/Pages/01042019.asp x

[2] https://en.wikipedia.org/wiki/Promissory_note

[3] https://www.reuters.com/article/us-venezuela-economy/venezuela-loosens-currency-exchange -controls-to-allow-forex-trading-idUSKCN1SD2NC

[4] Chapter: Reserve Currency Fallacy

[5] https://wiki.mises.org/wiki/Money_substitutes

Reserve Currency Fallacy

There is a theory that Bitcoin will eventually be held by states as a reserve currency[1] and that individuals will transact using monopoly money[2] "backed" by Bitcoin. The theory asserts that transaction volume is insufficient for its use as a consumer currency, but the ability to prevent monetary inflation[3] makes Bitcoin an ideal reserve asset. Central banks and their authorized functionaries would issue negotiable promissory notes[4] while holding Bitcoin in reserve. Given that Bitcoin cannot be inflated, the litany of problems produced by state control of money would be resolved, ushering in a new era of prosperity. Transaction fees would be low while transaction volume would be limitless.

Let us consider the scenario as it unfolds. Bitcoin becomes a fairly widely utilized currency[5] but struggles with low transaction volume, high fees and long confirmation times. In order to obtain a reserve of bitcoin (BTC) the state issues negotiable[6] Bitcoin Certificates (BC) in exchange for bitcoin. This may be accomplished by seizing centralized accounts (compelling conversion) or by market trading, both of which have been done to build gold reserves. An auditing process is set up whereby people can verify that the issued BC never exceeds BTC reserves. Legal tender laws[7] are created, requiring people to accept BC as payment for settlement of debts unless otherwise explicitly agreed. People purchase BC with BTC so that they can pay taxes and buy stuff from white market retailers. Eventually most BTC is held as state reserves.

Reference

[1] Chapter: Reservation Principle
[2] Chapter: Money Taxonomy
[3] https://en.wikipedia.org/wiki/Monetary_inflation
[4] https://en.wikipedia.org/wiki/Promissory_note
[5] https://en.wikipedia.org/wiki/Currency
[6] https://en.wikipedia.org/wiki/Negotiable_instrument
[7] https://en.wikipedia.org/wiki/Legal_tender

This scenario should sound familiar, as it is how states ended up with gold and people ended up with paper. The theory is invalid on multiple levels.

The ratio of issued BC to BTC in reserve cannot ever be effectively audited. Even if Bitcoin consensus rules somehow remain, there is *no way* to know how much BC has been issued, and there is no recourse if debasement is suspected. The central bank must be *trusted* to account for BC issuance, and ultimately this means everyone trusts the state to not engage in easing[1]. History demonstrates that this is unlikely, and nevertheless it is no improvement over current state monies.

So why is it that a person cannot ever effectively audit (validate) BC, as is possible with the BTC that it replaced? Because that would make BC indistinguishable from the BTC held in reserve. In other words the *reason* there is a difference between legal tender and reserve currency is to enable inflation of the currency in use (taxation[2]) while holding a better money[3] in reserve (hoard).

Furthermore, for Bitcoin to exist there must be an actual decentralized Bitcoin economy. Without individuals validating BTC received in trade, there is nobody to refuse invalid BTC as it comes to be redefined by the state[4]. In this case censorship[5] and inflation can easily be introduced, invalidating the theory. Only black market Bitcoin transaction and mining can resist[6] this transition. This provides little economic pressure on the state to maintain consistency with Bitcoin consensus rules.

Reference

[1] https://en.wikipedia.org/wiki/Quantitative_easing
[2] https://en.wikipedia.org/wiki/Seigniorage
[3] https://en.wikipedia.org/wiki/Gresham%27s_law
[4] Chapter: Fedcoin Objectives
[5] Chapter: Censorship Resistance Property
[6] Chapter: Axiom of Resistance

Layering preserves the cryptodynamic principles[1] of decentralization, while "backing" is full abandonment of them. Bitcoin cannot be sustained as predominantly a backing money for central bank notes. People must trade with it for it to be secure.

It is certainly possible for Bitcoin to be held by state treasuries, but this offers no transaction scaling or other advantage to people.

Reference

[1] Chapter: Cryptodynamic Principles

State Banking Principle

There is no actual lender of last resort[1] in free banking[2], it implies just another lender subject to the constraints demonstrated in Thin Air Fallacy[3]. However, in state banking this is the central bank[4], supported by the taxpayer. The state taxes to provide discount loans[5] to member banks[6] and the state treasury. The loans must be at a discount to market rates[7] as otherwise it doesn't constitute a last resort. Banks always have the option to borrow from other banks and potential depositors. Taxation is necessary to support the discount. So if the economic rate of interest is 10%, the state may lend to member banks at 3% and cover the difference with taxes.

The state has many sources of tax revenue, but typically central banks subsidize discounted loan rates with seigniorage[8]. Central banks are known for proclaiming that they do not "print money", but this is exactly what they do. The U.S. Federal Reserve[9] ("Fed") has the power to order new money[10] from the U.S. Treasury's Bureau of Engraving and Printing[11]. The Fed pays the printing cost[12] for "paper" money (actually cloth[13]) and face value for coinage[14]. The Treasury is just the contractor that performs the work.

Reference

[1] https://en.wikipedia.org/wiki/Lender_of_last_resort
[2] https://en.wikipedia.org/wiki/Free_banking
[3] Chapter: Thin Air Fallacy
[4] https://en.wikipedia.org/wiki/Central_bank
[5] https://en.wikipedia.org/wiki/Discount_window
[6] https://en.wikipedia.org/wiki/Structure_of_the_Federal_Reserve_System
[7] https://www.frbdiscountwindow.org/pages/discount-rates/current-discount-rates
[8] https://en.wikipedia.org/wiki/Seigniorage
[9] https://en.wikipedia.org/wiki/Federal_Reserve
[10] https://www.newyorkfed.org/aboutthefed/fedpoint/fed01.html
[11] https://www.moneyfactory.gov/
[12] https://www.federalreserve.gov/faqs/currency_12771.htm
[13] https://www.moneyfactory.gov/hmimpaperandink.html
[14] https://en.wikipedia.org/wiki/Coin

Typically coinage is produced such that it has slightly higher face value than use value[1], in order to prevent disappearance[2] of the coins. This use value must therefore be reduced when face value declines relative to it, as the result of devaluation of the corresponding fiat.

This implies that the monetary inflation[3] of state fiat is literally the consequence of printing the "paper" money. This process is somewhat obscured. The Fed does not first print the money, stuff it in a vault, and then lend it out. This is unnecessary. The order is reversed in practice. The Fed issues discounted loans, with the *presumption* of money in its vault.

The settlement process established by the Fed maintains track of how much money is in each member bank's reserve. The bulk of settlements can often be netted[4], but periodically money must be physically moved.

To further reduce transportation costs, a significant portion of member bank reserves are required to be held in the Fed's own vault. This can be achieved by purchasing Treasury securities (Treasuries[5]) that are offered for sale[6] by the Fed. These are money substitutes[7] considered sufficient to satisfy member bank reserve requirements. Treasuries are debt issued by the U.S. Treasury and generally purchased in bulk on the open market[8] by the Fed. The Fed reduces the yield of Treasuries (i.e. the rate of interest paid by the state) by providing increased demand. It funds these operations in the same

Reference

[1] https://en.wikipedia.org/wiki/Use_value

[2] https://en.wikipedia.org/wiki/Gresham%27s_law

[3] https://en.wikipedia.org/wiki/Monetary_inflation

[4] https://en.wikipedia.org/wiki/Set-off_(law)#Close_out_netting

[5] https://en.wikipedia.org/wiki/United_States_Treasury_security

[6] https://www.stlouisfed.org/in-plain-english/a-closer-look-at-open-market-operations

[7] https://wiki.mises.org/wiki/Money_substitutes

[8] https://fred.stlouisfed.org/series/TREAST

essential manner as discounted loans to its member banks. The distinction is merely that these purchases are discounted loans to the state.

The Fed can *pretend* it has money in its vault and print it only as required for settlement. This creates the illusion of monetary inflation being the result of lending. But it is actually entirely the result of the Fed's ability to purchase money at a discount, thereby funding the loans. When a member bank requires money it can buy it from the Fed using Treasuries. When the Fed's reserve of actual money is insufficient, it simply makes a "withdrawal" from the taxpayer by ordering money from the printer.

The Fed pays the Treasury the following amounts for dollar "bills":

Denomination	Price
$1	5.5 cents
$2	5.5 cents
$5	11.4 cents
$10	11.1 cents
$20	11.5 cents
$50	11.5 cents
$100	14.2 cents

If it had cost 5.5 cents to print a $1 bill in 1915, it would now cost about $1.40 to do so. When the cost of printing a bill reaches its face value, it has transitioned from fiat to commodity money[1]. At that point its seigniorage value is zero. As devaluation continues the denomination must be discontinued. Observation of central banks engaged in

Reference

[1] https://en.wikipedia.org/wiki/Commodity_money

hyperinflation[1] is informative, as money reaches printing cost over much shorter periods of time, and coins tend to disappear entirely. Issuance of larger denomination notes allows the money to remain fiat as the commodity money is abandoned. The Zimbabwe Dollar[2] reached 100,000,000,000,000 unit bills before it was abandoned entirely in favor of foreign currencies.

Without this ability to create fiat the Fed would be unable to settle accounts, just as would any bank, if there was insufficient reserve (including that which could be borrowed) to cover withdrawals and defaults. Until the member bank must settle in money, such as in the case of cash withdrawal at ATMs[3], teller windows[4] or with non-member banks and other institutions, there is no need to move the actual money, or print it.

But without the ability to print it below cost, the Fed would be subject to default just as any other bank.

The total amount of U.S. Dollars in circulation[5] is referred to as "M0". This includes all tangible currency ("vault cash") plus intangible bank balances in Federal Reserve accounts. These two forms are considered interchangeable "obligations"[6] (money) of the Fed. The intangible obligations are money that is accounted for but not yet printed.

As borrowing by member banks is reduced, such as by the Fed raising its interest rates, the Fed's obligations can be destroyed with the opposite effect of its printing. While the

Reference

[1] https://en.wikipedia.org/wiki/Hyperinflation_in_Venezuelahttps:/en.wikipedia.org/wiki/Zimbabwean_dollar

[2] https://en.wikipedia.org/wiki/Zimbabwean_dollar

[3] https://en.wikipedia.org/wiki/Automated_teller_machine

[4] https://en.wikipedia.org/wiki/Bank_teller

[5] https://en.wikipedia.org/wiki/Money_supply#United_States

[6] https://en.wikipedia.org/wiki/Money_supply#Money_creation_by_commercial_banks

Fed has contracted M0[1] by almost 20% in the four years since its peak in 2015, this comes at a cost to tax revenue. The Fed masquerades as a non-profit organization, remitting net income from its loans to the U.S. Treasury[2] annually.

> The Federal Reserve increased the federal funds rate target seven times since between Dec. 2015 and June 2018. This has implications for the path of the federal deficit and federal debt in two ways:
>
> * Directly through net interest payments
> * Indirectly through the yearly remittances from the Fed to the U.S. Treasury Department
>
> The yearly remittances to the Treasury are essentially the leftover Fed revenue after operating expenses. By law, this additional revenue must be turned over to the Treasury.
>
> The revenue sent to the Treasury peaked at $97.7 billion in 2015 and has been steadily falling since. In January, the Fed sent $80.2 billion to the Treasury.
>
> *Federal Reserve Bank of St. Louis*

This "leftover Fed revenue" is that which is earned, after operating expenses, from loans of money printed by the U.S. Treasury at nominal cost, guaranteed by its monopoly protection[3] in doing so. So the net result is that the Treasury prints new money and then recaptures the money earned as interest on that money printed. As shown above, the Treasury also borrows money at discounted rates indirectly financed by the Fed, through the issuance of Treasury securities. **While money is not printed and then deposited directly into the Treasury, the result is the same.**

State monopoly money[4] is not created *ex nihilo* by fraudulent bank accounting. It is literally created from old blue jeans[5] by the state.

Reference

[1] https://tradingeconomics.com/united-states/money-supply-m0

[2] https://www.stlouisfed.org/on-the-economy/2018/september/fed-payments-treasury-rising-interest-rates

[3] https://en.wikipedia.org/wiki/Counterfeit

[4] Chapter: Money Taxonomy

[5] https://www.washingtonpost.com/news/wonk/wp/2013/12/16/how-tight-jeans-almost-ruined-americas-money

The transition to a modern "cashless society"[1] implies that central banks would retain the existing form of accounting for not-yet-printed fiat, and simply perform all settlement internally. This eliminates printing and settlement transportation costs, and ensures full censorability. An instance of Fedcoin[2], such as the experimental e-Krona[3], would be required for people to transact with state money electronically. Bitcoin serves the same purpose, but without state control over either issuance (mining) or confirmation. For these reasons Bitcoin cannot be expected to act as the reserve currency[4] (money) for state banking, as it would necessarily follow the same trajectory as the failed gold standard[5]. Bitcoin's value proposition[6] is in the avoidance of state money.

Reference

[1] https://www.nytimes.com/2018/11/21/business/sweden-cashless-society.html

[2] Chapter: Fedcoin Objectives

[3] https://www.riksbank.se/en-gb/payments--cash/e-krona

[4] Chapter: Reserve Currency Fallacy

[5] https://en.wikipedia.org/wiki/Gold_standard

[6] Chapter: Value Proposition

MINING

ASIC Monopoly Fallacy

There is a theory that Bitcoin ASIC[1] price is controlled by a cartel[2] of miners, creating a disproportionate advantage to mining partners of the cartel.

There is no economic difference between a cartel and a single organization. Changing organizational size is a free market outcome observable as capital seeks optimal economies of scale[3]. If partners receive ASICs at a price that produces a below market return on capital, it amounts to an internal subsidy between partners. The same is true of a price that produces an above market return on capital, with the subsidy in the opposite direction. As such there is no net advantage to such discounting between partners.

Production is generally set at a level intended to produce a maximum rate of return[4] on capital. The only economically rational way for a producer to raise price is to limit production below that optimum. Otherwise higher price implies unsold inventory, resulting in lower net returns. This implies that production must be restricted by the cartel in order to raise unit price[5] for non-partners.

Limiting production leaves an opportunity for other producers to capture customers with a lower marginal utility[6] for the product, as those customers would otherwise be unserved. Thus competition lowers price until the market clears. A free market seeks the clearing price that produces the global return on capital (interest). A current price above

Reference

[1] https://en.wikipedia.org/wiki/Application-specific_integrated_circuit
[2] https://mises.org/library/man-economy-and-state-power-and-market/html/p/1059
[3] https://en.wikipedia.org/wiki/Economies_of_scale
[4] https://en.wikipedia.org/wiki/Rate_of_return
[5] https://en.wikipedia.org/wiki/Unit_price
[6] https://en.wikipedia.org/wiki/Marginal_utility

this level increases production and below decreases production. It is time preference[1] that determines the rate of interest.

Unless production is disproportionately subject to anti-market forces, such as tax or subsidy, everyone enjoys the same opportunity to raise capital and compete in production.

If competition does not arise it implies that returns on this line of business are at least consistent with average market returns. Tax and subsidy cause regional distortions but do not eliminate competition. **In other words, monopoly price is only achievable by state grant of monopoly power.**

A related theory asserts that purchasing ASICs from this cartel increases its hash power. This is invalid on the basis of the above explanation of monopolistic pricing. The producer's capital will seek the same return in any line of business or investment. There is no reason to believe that the return will be disproportionate in ASICs.

A related theory asserts that the Bitcoin proof-of-work algorithm produces a pooling pressure[2], as a consequence of the supposed cartelization. If people truly believe that ASICs are overpriced the rational response is to raise capital and produce ASICs. But in any case, market and anti-market (state) forces alone control chip production and as such it does not constitute a protocol-based pooling pressure.

Reference

[1] https://en.wikipedia.org/wiki/Time_preference
[2] Chapter: Pooling Pressure Risk

Balance of Power Fallacy

Power in Bitcoin rests with miners and merchants. Yet these two powers are not "balanced" between each other, as if locked in some sort of checks-and-balances[1] system. Miner power is orthogonal[2] to merchant power. Miners control transaction selection, merchants control validity, and neither can control the other. Not surprisingly, in the original description[3] and implementation these roles were combined.

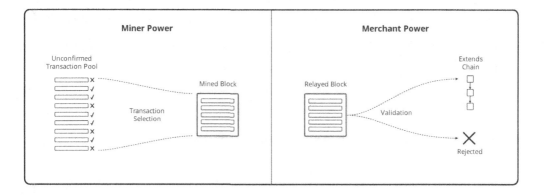

Power is not the same as influence. Merchants can influence miners by not buying the service. Miners can similarly influence merchants by not producing it. These choices manifest as splits or stalls. However the nature of power is that it can (and often does) ignore influence. The state has power; it can apply coercion and co-option while ignoring influence. Merchants and miners *together* have the power to defend[4] against these aggressions, but neither can do so without the support of the other.

Reference

[1] https://en.wikipedia.org/wiki/Separation_of_powers
[2] https://en.wikipedia.org/wiki/Orthogonality
[3] https://bitcoin.org/bitcoin.pdf
[4] Chapter: Risk Sharing Principle

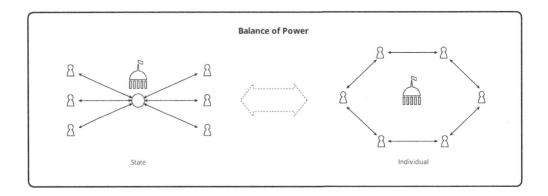

Balance of Power

State

Individual

The balance of power in Bitcoin is between *individuals* and the state. Even states create systems that attempt[1] to isolate their moneys from political control. Bitcoin is no different in that sense, incorporating the resistance axiom[2]. Individuals can be miners and can be merchants. With broad distribution of these activities it becomes difficult for state actors to censor this market. **The idea that miners and merchants are in an adversarial position is a failure to understand the Bitcoin security model.**

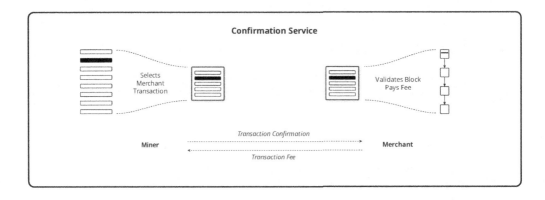

Confirmation Service

Selects
Merchant
Transaction

Validates Block
Pays Fee

Transaction Confirmation

Miner

Merchant

Transaction Fee

Merchants purchase a service from miners and as such the two are engaged in trade. Merchants purchase mining services that conform to their rules for a satisfactory fee. They are free to split and miners are free to not mine at all, or to not select particular

Reference

[1] https://www.federalreserve.gov/aboutthefed/bios/board/default.htm

[2] Chapter: Axiom of Resistance

transactions for whatever reason suits them. Trade is neither adversarial nor asymmetrical, it is voluntary and mutually-beneficial, with all tensions resolved in price.

This failure in understanding leads people to believe that mining can be centrally pooled as long as merchants are not centralized in validation, as the economy can control the behavior of mining, rendering the system secure. This belief is incorrect but unfortunately people are drawing this invalid conclusion[1] from recent events. A closely-related fallacy[2] is that a proof-of-work hard fork by merchants can control miner behavior.

Reference

[1] https://www.coindesk.com/uasf-revisited-will-bitcoins-user-revolt-leave-lasting-legacy
[2] Chapter: Proof of Work Fallacy

Byproduct Mining Fallacy

There is a theory that, to the extent Bitcoin mining can consume a necessary and otherwise unmarketable byproduct[1] of energy production, such as unused natural gas[2], a reduction in marketable energy consumption is implied.

Given a new byproduct market, not taking advantage of the presumed lower price represents opportunity cost[3] to each miner. Competition for the byproduct increases its price, eventually up to the level where the net advantage is eliminated. In the interim this represents a mining profit opportunity[4].

Paradoxically[5], any reduced cost results in proportionally greater consumption. The reduced cost of mining must result in increased mining so that its cost returns to the reward level. So the byproduct formerly "consumed" as waste increases mining hash rate until the same cost is consumed in mining. Net mining energy consumption is actually increased by the lower price.

Yet in monetizing a waste resource, the overall marketable energy supply is increased without an increase in its production cost. And demand for the otherwise marketable energy supply in mining is decreased. This implies a reduced market energy price.

A corresponding expansion of production generally may result from a reduced market energy price. This price stability[6] is a general characteristic of all products. **As such a consequent reduction in overall energy consumption from byproduct mining cannot**

Reference

[1] https://en.m.wikipedia.org/wiki/Waste
[2] https://en.m.wikipedia.org/wiki/Gas_flare
[3] https://en.wikipedia.org/wiki/Opportunity_cost
[4] https://bitcoinist.com/bitcoin-mining-waste-oil-industry
[5] Chapter: Efficiency Paradox
[6] Chapter: Stability Property

be assumed, invalidating the theory. However, an overall increase in wealth is implied by greater production at the same cost or same production at lower cost.

Causation Fallacy

There is a theory that mining "follows" price, or more specifically, reward value. The implication is that mining is slaved to price, lacking any input into coin utility.

Consider the miner who responds only to historical reward values. This person cannot be the first miner, because the reward has no historical value. No price can be established because no trades have occurred. The miner might have heard that a number of unconfirmed units bought a pizza, but maybe the same units are double-spent. He must anticipate a certain level of future net return on capital that is unknowable until it either materializes, or does not. This is the nature of entrepreneurial risk. The risk must be taken before the product can exist. One might believe that the risk can be shifted to the consumer, with advance ordering. But at that point the consumer has become the entrepreneur, providing the capital for, and assuming the risk of, production.

It is certainly possible for a miner to respond only to historical reward values once history has been established by someone else's risk-taking. But what is the time window and method of averaging that predicts future reward values? The unique ability to predict exchange prices would provide the miner unlimited riches. If it could be done generally, price would never change, as all potential changes would be discounted upon first minting. So either price changes unpredictably, or not at all. In other words, every miner faces the same situation as the first. Historical prices do not exist that can predict future prices.

Assuming a market average return on mining capital generally, both overestimation and underestimation of reward value imply loss in relation to the cost of capital. Given the nature of competition, profits and losses (above and below market returns on capital respectively) experience constant negative existential pressure. In other words, the market attempts to eliminate these errors. But given the unpredictable nature of price, it can never actually do so. Production never seeks demand that exists, which is inherently historical, it always seeks demand that it anticipates. **Production continues to guess at future consumption and in doing so creates the opportunity for consumption.**

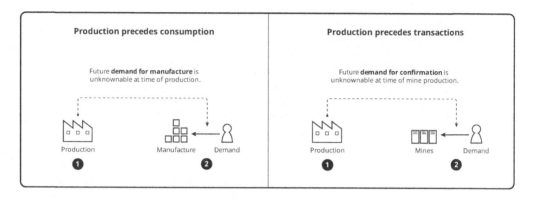

Miners trade their capital for units of bitcoin. In doing so they are a fraction of the overall demand for bitcoin. Yes miners do not independently establish price. Their particular demand is no more impactful on price than is that of a non-miner with the same level of demand.

One could say that miners converge on a market return on capital by anticipating *highest* possible fee values. But merchants similarly converge on a market return on miner capital by seeking the *lowest* possible fee value. However, miners must anticipate overall demand and risk mining before there can be any utility. So to the extent that there is any asymmetry, mining precedes transacting, just as all production must precede consumption. Assuming otherwise conflates the direction a market seeks with the manner in which it does so.

Decoupled Mining Fallacy

There is a theory that security[1] is increased by decoupling reward from transaction selection in pooled mining. The theory holds that by sharing only the reward, control over transaction selection shifts to miners with less hash power. This implies a reduction in the variance discount[2] and therefore an increase in the competitiveness[3] of smaller mines. Because smaller mines can presumably operate more covertly than larger, this in turn implies that censorship resistance[4] is increased.

The theory fails to recognize that control over transaction selection remains with the pool operator and is therefore invalid. The sole benefit is variance reduction, but this is only realized by the receipt of payment. As payment is discretionary any condition may be attached. Such conditions may include censorship and identity. Member recourse is to leave the pool for another, just as with a coupled pool. As such decoupled pools and coupled pools are equally subject to co-option.

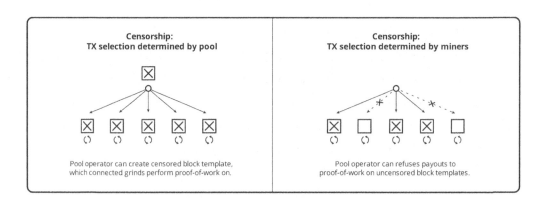

Censorship: TX selection determined by pool	Censorship: TX selection determined by miners
Pool operator can create censored block template, which connected grinds perform proof-of-work on.	Pool operator can refuses payouts to proof-of-work on uncensored block templates.

Reference

[1] Chapter: Qualitative Security Model

[2] Chapter: Variance Discount Flaw

[3] Chapter: Censorship Resistance Property

[4] Chapter: Axiom of Resistance

There is a related theory that transparency of a decoupled pool is greater than that of a coupled pool, facilitating flight of members to non-censoring pools, therefore limiting the dominance of censoring pools. Generously accepting the assumptions of greater transparency and independent miners operating against financial self-interest, we are still left with the fact of co-option. The state can still reserve for itself the ability to operate with the financial advantages of pooling[1] and the theory is therefore invalid.

This fallacy is similar to the Relay Fallacy[2] in that all financial advantage depends on otherwise independent miners granting control over that advantage to a single person.

Reference

[1] Chapter: Pooling Pressure Risk

[2] Chapter: Relay Fallacy

Dedicated Cost Principle

Unnecessary costs incurred by miners contribute nothing to either double-spend resistance or censorship resistance[1]. Such costs constitute true waste, representing nothing more than a given miner's inefficiency. For example, it does not contribute to security if a miner with misconfigured machines expends a great deal of energy while being unable to win a reward due to the misconfiguration. Any cost that is not strictly required for the optimal generation of hash power is not a necessary cost. A misconfiguration by one miner does not represent cost to another.

There is a theory that proof-of-work (PoW) can be made more energy efficient[2] by introducing non-dedicated costs to the mining function. One such example is the discovery of prime numbers[3]. The reason to incorporate such costs is that the resulting discoveries have presumed marketable value. If not there would objectively be no value in the incorporation.

By analogy, brewers can sell their grain byproducts to farmers. This improves their efficiency by reducing cost. So to the extent that the resulting byproduct is valuable, its production does not incur a net cost. Yet necessary net cost must rise to the level of reward, as a consequence of competition. Therefore the same result would be achieved by basic PoW consuming the full reward value and independent energy-consuming operations generating the marketable products. **Any cost dedicated to the production of independently-marketable value can be offset by selling that byproduct.** As such the theory is invalid.

Reference

[1] Chapter: Censorship Resistance Property
[2] Chapter: Efficiency Paradox
[3] http://primecoin.io

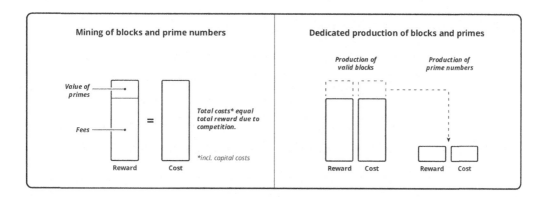

Merged mining[1] is typically implemented to resolve the problem of bootstrapping a new coin past the vulnerable stage of low hash rate. This design fails to recognize that hash rate not dedicated to the new coin does not contribute to its security. As the full cost of the hash rate can be recouped by selling it on one chain, there is no cost to censor the other merge-mined chain(s).

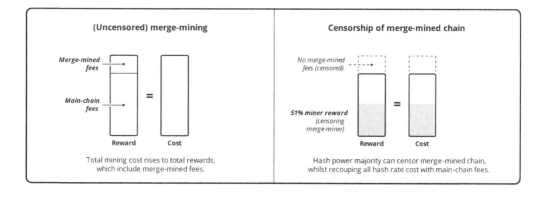

Reference

[1] https://eprint.iacr.org/2017/791.pdf

Efficiency Paradox

Bitcoin mining overall cannot be made more efficient in terms of real cost. Given that all costs resolve to energy, this could be restated as, Bitcoin cannot be made more energy efficient. Paradoxically[1], no matter what technology improvement is introduced, the cost of transaction confirmation remains the sum of the reward for confirmation.

This apparent contradiction arises from the fact that reward ultimately determines cost. An increase in hash rate for the same cost results in a difficulty increase to maintain the block period, increasing cost accordingly. Bitcoin mining must always consume in cost the amount of its current reward.

Reference

[1] https://en.wikipedia.org/wiki/Paradox

Empty Block Fallacy

There is a theory that the mining of empty blocks is an attack. The theory does not require that the blocks are mined on a weak branch in an attempt to enable double-spending, nor does it specify what person is attacked.

Consider the following:

- The term "attack" implies theft. The Bitcoin whitepaper[1], for example, uses the term only to describe double-spend attempts.

- A reward consists of fees for transactions and a subsidy for the block. The miner who forgoes transaction fees by not including transactions is not rewarded for them.

- The miner's hash power contributes proportionally to the security of the network. The subsidy is compensation for that security during the inflationary phase. The purpose of inflation is to rationally distribute units. The rational distribution is specifically in exchange for hash power, not for transaction inclusion.

- Transaction confirmation is not assured. Fees are the incentive for confirmation. Lack of confirmation objectively implies insufficient fee.

- Empty block mining is entirely consistent with consensus rules and cannot be reasonably prevented by a new rule.

Furthermore, if 10% of the hash power mines empty blocks, then confirmations will take 10% longer on average. Yet if a miner removes 10% of the total hash power, confirmations will also take 10% longer on average, until the next difficulty adjustment. Mining an empty block is therefore indistinguishable from not mining.

Reference

[1] https://bitcoin.org/bitcoin.pdf

It is worth exploring the source of the fallacy. Because of the Zero Sum Property[1], there may be an assumption that mining an empty block "unfairly" takes away the opportunity for transactions to be confirmed.

A miner commits capital to mining, producing hash power. Setting aside the effects of pooling[2], the miner is subsidized in proportion to hash rate. Without this work other miners would produce the same average number of blocks at proportionally lower difficulty. In other words, *actual* attacks would be proportionally cheaper. So despite not being rewarded for including transactions, the empty block miner is securing previously-confirmed transactions.

Given that the marginal cost[3] of including a transaction is necessarily below average fee levels, the empty block miner is suffering an opportunity cost[4]. This amounts to the miner subsidizing the security of the chain.

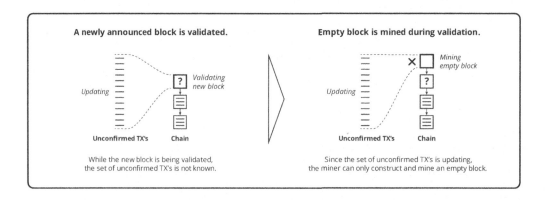

A newly announced block is validated.

Updating — Validating new block

Unconfirmed TX's   Chain

While the new block is being validated,
the set of unconfirmed TX's is not known.

Empty block is mined during validation.

Mining empty block

Updating —

Unconfirmed TX's   Chain

Since the set of unconfirmed TX's is updating,
the miner can only construct and mine an empty block.

Reference

[1] Chapter: Zero Sum Property

[2] Chapter: Pooling Pressure Risk

[3] https://en.wikipedia.org/wiki/Marginal_cost

[4] https://en.wikipedia.org/wiki/Opportunity_cost

While this seems economically irrational, it can be otherwise due to the offsetting opportunity cost for waiting on a new non-empty candidate following an announcement. **To the extent that it reduces miner costs, empty block mining can have no impact on either fees or confirmation rate.** The theory is therefore invalid.

While a given miner may consider it advantageous to mine empty blocks, it is within every other person's power to do otherwise. It is ultimately the exercise of this competitive and self-interested opportunity that secures the coin, against actual attacks.

Energy Exhaustion Fallacy

There is a theory that proof-of-work may exhaust all energy available to people. PoW converts energy into a monotonically increasing[1] double-spend barrier for any given transaction. This is comparable to the energy expended in securing any money against counterfeit (by its own issuer or otherwise).

The purpose of any security measure is to create a cost necessary to overcome the measure, i.e. a financial barrier. Bitcoin creates its double-spend barrier by compelling the attacker to replace the branch of the targeted transaction with one of probabilistically greater work. Interestingly, such a replacement raises the barrier to subsequent attackers. **The energy expended is not independently important, the erected barrier is the attacker's necessary financial burden.**

The security barrier (S) of a block is the product of unit hash cost (C), hash rate (H), and period (T).

```
S = C * H * T
```

The adjustment varies hash rate to maintain a constant period for a given hash cost and security.

```
T = S / (C * H)
```

Reference

[1] https://en.wikipedia.org/wiki/Monotonic_function

A constant period implies that hash rate is inversely proportional to cost for a given security.

$$H \sim S / C$$

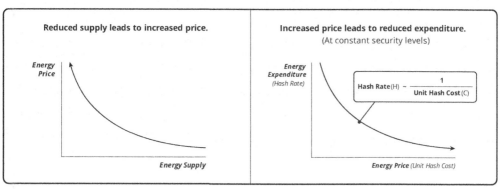

Reduced supply leads to increased price.

Energy Price

Energy Supply

Increased price leads to reduced expenditure.
(At constant security levels)

Energy Expenditure
(Hash Rate)

$$\text{Hash Rate}(H) \sim \frac{1}{\text{Unit Hash Cost}(C)}$$

Energy Price (Unit Hash Cost)

As energy supply is reduced its price must increase, which reduces the amount expended for a given level of security. Therefore energy cannot be exhausted by mining and the theory is invalid.

Energy Store Fallacy

There is a theory that the value of energy expended by proof-of-work is converted to coin value, in effect "storing" the energy for later consumption. Assuming that energy and the coin have value to people at some future time, they can again be traded.

Yet this is at best a poor metaphor. Miners trade energy for units. However *all* merchants who accept units of the coin trade something for it, and *all things* offered in trade represent demand. The theory errs in the implication that energy value expended in mining is unique in its contribution to value. **Apart from magnitude, one source of demand cannot be a generally greater determinant of value than another**. As such the theory is invalid.

Furthermore, it is a similar error to assert that money[1] is a store of value[2]. Money is a store of money. Only objects can actually be stored. The value of money derives entirely from the value of what it can be traded for, to the people trading. As value is subjective[3], it is human preference, subject to constant and unpredictable change, and cannot be stored.

Reference

[1] Chapter: Money Taxonomy

[2] https://en.m.wikipedia.org/wiki/Store_of_value

[3] https://en.wikipedia.org/wiki/Subjective_theory_of_value

Energy Waste Fallacy

There is a theory that proof-of-work wastes energy. This implies that the level of security provided is greater than necessary, or the same level of security can be provided by another externalized proof at a lower energy cost. An *internalized* proof, specifically proof-of-stake[1], is a different security model which is not cryptodynamically secure[2], and is not considered here.

Total hash power is a function of reward, which is a function of fees, which are determined by the confirmation market. If a person considers current hash power insufficient to secure trade at a given value against double-spend then the depth requirement increases. Additionally, as shown in Utility Threshold Property[3], transactions with insufficient value for even single confirmation security are priced out of the chain.

These upper and lower security bounds depend on confirmation cost and are therefore independent of the proof technique. **There is no necessary level of security, just a subjective confirmation depth and minimum utility.**

Confirmation security increases with the cost of generating each block. The double-spend of a transaction requires that its branch be superseded by another with a probabilistically greater cost. So energy cost can be reduced only by expending the same average cost for a given confirmation time, but with a lower energy component.

Work incurs cost in several forms, including labor, hardware, services, land, etc. Any other externalized proof consumes these same resources, though potentially in different

Reference

[1] https://en.wikipedia.org/wiki/Proof-of-stake
[2] Chapter: Proof of Stake Fallacy
[3] Chapter: Utility Threshold Property

proportion. The question of energy cost reduction is therefore reduced to whether an energy component of the cost of a proof can be replaced by another resource component with the same cost. However the cost of the substitute resource includes all of its production costs, which must resolve to energy. The theory is therefore invalid.

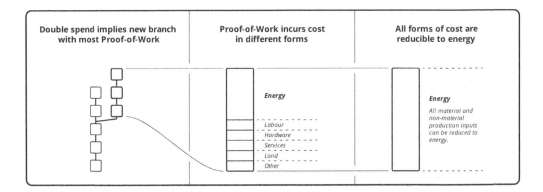

| Double spend implies new branch with most Proof-of-Work | Proof-of-Work incurs cost in different forms | All forms of cost are reducible to energy |

Additionally, securing any coin incurs a cost to merchants. As such the fact of its use by them implies that it is preferred over alternatives. This implies the alternatives are ultimately more costly. As all costs are fundamentally resolved in energy consumption, it follows that the money[1] in use is the most energy efficient.

Reference

[1] Chapter: Money Taxonomy

Fee Recovery Fallacy

There is a theory that miners gain financial advantage over other miners by mining their own transactions and "recovering" their own fees.

The theory ignores the opportunity cost[1] of mining block space without collecting payment for it. Payment of a fee *of any amount* to one's self is a financial non-event. Failure to collect a fee is a real cost in the amount forgone, as the cost of mining that portion of the block is uncompensated. **The actual fee paid by the miner is the opportunity forgone.**

There is a related theory that fee estimation tools may be fooled into recommending higher fees than are required. As shown in Side Fee Fallacy[2] this assumes a relationship between historical and future fee rates that does not exist, and that all fees are visible on chain, which is not the case.

Reference

[1] https://en.m.wikipedia.org/wiki/Opportunity_cost
[2] Chapter: Side Fee Fallacy

Halving Fallacy

Bitcoin consensus rules produce a predictable rate of monetary inflation. This rate is reduced periodically at a point called the halving. There are several step functions[1] in Bitcoin. The halving occurs every 210,000 strong blocks, the difficulty adjustment every 2,016 strong blocks and chain organization approximately every 10 minutes. The numeric values that control these intervals are arbitrary, yet the discontinuity is necessary due to the discrete intervals required for proof-of-work. There is a theory that the halving creates a financial cliff for miners that may lead to a perpetual stall. The theory is based on the confluence of two step functions (halving and difficulty), causing the period of another (organization) to expand dramatically due to coincident reduction in miner profits.

The theory assumes that the difficulty adjustment resets average miner financial profit[2] to zero, allowing only the top half of miners (by profitability) to survive, eventually reducing mining to just a few miners. In other words the difficulty adjustment is considered a positive pooling pressure[3]. However there is no reason to believe that the adjustment reduces *any* miner's profit to zero. The consequence of the assumption is not that there will be *few* miners, but that there will be *none*, due to the difficulty adjustment alone. The adjustment actually does nothing to regulate miner profits, it controls only the organization period. With no adjustment, profit would be unaffected while the organization period and therefore variance would respond to total hash rate. Time preference[4], which dictates market return on capital, regulates miner profits just as it does in every market.

Reference

[1] https://en.wikipedia.org/wiki/Step_function
[2] http://www.investopedia.com/terms/e/economicprofit.asp
[3] Chapter: Pooling Pressure Risk
[4] https://en.wikipedia.org/wiki/Time_preference

Consider the case of no price change. In this case there is no reason to expect a change in total hash rate, no adjustments to difficulty, and we can conclude that the average mine generates the market return on capital. In other words any number of independent miners can compete indefinitely (absent actual pooling pressures).

Consider also that price changes, difficulty adjustments, and reward fluctuations all effect miner profitability in the same manner. A difficulty adjustment and/or halving is therefore no more important to a miner than a comparable price fluctuation, and exhibits greater predictability.

The theory also contemplates that reward may be insufficient to compensate miners for difficulty immediately following a halving. As such they may opt to reduce hash rate, extending confirmation times until fees rise, price rises and/or difficulty adjusts downward. Yet fees and price are determined in a market and can certainly rise to any level that people are willing to pay.

There is no way to know what levels the market will support, but price continues to have a much greater impact than halvings. The largest halvings have passed with no disruption. Given that subsequent halvings will produce the equivalent of an exponentially *lesser* price reduction, there is no reason to believe future events will be any more interesting than past.

Impotent Mining Fallacy

There is a theory that miners have no power. This is distinct from the closely related Proof of Work Fallacy[1]. The theory rests on the assumption that miners are subject to economic pressures that preclude sustained effective attacks. This theory leads people to believe that mining can be strongly pooled as long as merchants are not centralized, as the economy can control the behavior of mining, rendering the system secure. The consequence of this invalid theory is complacency regarding the insecurity caused by pooling.

The theory holds that if majority hash power double-spends then merchants will necessarily increase confirmation depth requirements, increasing the cost of subsequent attacks. At some point an equilibrium is reached where greater depths are considered sufficient for exchange. Given that this would preclude double spending altogether, there would be no advantage to sustaining the attack. The theory accepts that attacks can happen, but not frequently enough to materially reduce utility.

The theory also holds that a miner cannot avoid selecting the highest fee transactions as this reduces relative reward, enriching other miners. This is presumed to lead to a loss of majority power and therefore an inability to continue. This aspect of the theory implies that miners cannot effectively censor.

The theory also considers that selfish mining by majority hash power is feasible, but in the absence of double-spending and censorship, there is no adverse consequence to the economy. In this case the majority simply becomes the one miner as all others are unable to retain rewards. Despite lack of competition, hash rate and fee levels are maintained by the ever-looming *possibility* of competition.

Reference

[1] Chapter: Proof of Work Fallacy

Yet miners and merchants are trading partners, engaged voluntarily in mutually-beneficial activity. As explored in the Balance of Power Fallacy[1], neither can control the other and price is the resolution of all preferences. This would seem to support the theory, however **the theory does not address the threat**, and is actually a red herring[2]. Bitcoin is designed to defend against *non-market* forces, specifically the state. Market forces are never a threat to the market itself.

The pooling of hash power eviscerates security, as states can simply co-opt it. But states can also build their own mines to the same effect. Bitcoin therefore requires both significant hash power *and* distribution of that power among people who are willing and able to risk state controls[3].

The state is an economically rational actor. Inflation is profitable for the issuer. Bitcoin's widespread use would prevent states from effectively levying the inflation tax[4]. State attacks are therefore expected, and analogous attacks are commonplace[5]. It is practically inevitable that states will subsidize attacks, but even the possibility invalidates the theory.

Reference

[1] Chapter: Balance of Power Fallacy
[2] https://en.wikipedia.org/wiki/Red_herring
[3] Chapter: Risk Sharing Principle
[4] https://en.wikipedia.org/wiki/Seigniorage
[5] https://en.wikipedia.org/wiki/Foreign_exchange_controls

Miner Business Model

Miners play a zero sum game[1] within a positive sum[2] economy. They compete with each other, not the economy. Rising utility is the reflection of a positive sum and a natural consequence of trade.

It has been argued that blocks mined in a period of rising price produce outsized returns for miners, at least until the difficulty adjustment. This idea is based on the common failure to understand that market prices are not predictable[3]. Wagers on price change are speculative. There is no reason to assume that Bitcoin speculation is any more or less effective than any other. To the extent that a rising price is generally predictable by miners, competition predict its, invalidating the idea of any inherent outsized return.

Bitcoin mining investment on the other hand is based on the predictable relationship between profit and competition over time. That relationship predicts that the average of all mining approaches the market rate of interest. As with all markets, shorter time periods are unpredictable in price and longer periods approach market returns. Ultimately time preference[4] controls the market rate of investment return.

So how does a miner achieve outsized returns? It cannot be done with side fee agreements[5]. There is only one way to make a higher-than-market rate of return, which is to have a below average cost of hash power for the coin. This is achieved by either taking advantage of pooling pressures[6] or through superior operational efficiency.

Reference

[1] https://en.wikipedia.org/wiki/Zero-sum_game
[2] https://en.wikipedia.org/wiki/Win-win_game
[3] https://en.wikipedia.org/wiki/Chaos_theory
[4] https://en.wikipedia.org/wiki/Time_preference
[5] Chapter: Side Fee Fallacy
[6] Chapter: Pooling Pressure Risk

Because of the zero sum property[1], these are offset by lower-than-market rates of return by other miners. The premium therefore declines for an honest miner above 50% hash power, to zero at 100%.

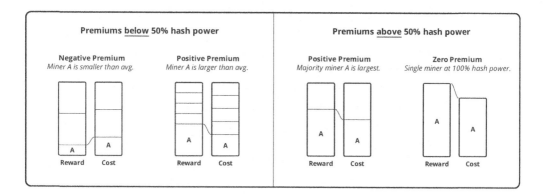

However other miners will eventually exit as their capital seeks market returns. This would leave one miner, bound to market returns. In other words, making outsized returns requires others from whom to capture those returns. The highest return that can be sustained is a function of the greatest opportunity cost others are willing to sustain. This is a function of differential reward utility, as discussed in Threat Level Paradox[2].

By limiting dividends[3] to market rates of return and reinvesting all remaining reward, a miner can maintain a constant hash power and thereby obtain market returns against a capital base proportional to Bitcoin capitalization. Reinvesting dividends increases hash power and liquidation decreases it. Grinds are liquidated by taking each device offline as it becomes a net negative producer, or discounting[4] those future returns by selling the device.

Reference

[1] Chapter: Zero Sum Property
[2] Chapter: Threat Level Paradox
[3] https://en.wikipedia.org/wiki/Dividend
[4] https://en.wikipedia.org/wiki/Present_value

Mining rate of return on capital is dependent on time preference alone. The relationship between the economy and miners is further explored in Balance of Power Fallacy[1].

Reference

[1] Chapter: Balance of Power Fallacy

Pooling Pressure Risk

Pooling pressure is the set of financial incentives for hash rate aggregation, specifically:

- Proximity Premium[1]
- Variance Discount[2]
- Market Variation
- Market Distortion
- Economies of Scale[3]

Latency and variance are unavoidable. The consensus rules actually create these first two financial incentives. Variation is a consequence of varying market price for mining resources. Distortion is a consequence of varying non-market costs including tax, regulation, subsidy, and patent; the force that Bitcoin is intended to resist[4]. In a high threat environment economies of scale may become negative due to the cost associated with greater visibility[5] but may otherwise be positive.

There are several manifestations of pooling. One is geographic, where independent miners become physically closer together. Another is cooperative, where formerly independent miners join forces and co-locate grinding. Another is virtual, where miners become grinders and aggregate hash rate to a single remote miner. Another is the use of relays[6], which aggregate miner hash power. Another is capital flow, since the higher hash rate associated with greater capital utilization is a form of co-location.

Reference

[1] Chapter: Proximity Premium Flaw

[2] Chapter: Variance Discount Flaw

[3] https://en.wikipedia.org/wiki/Economies_of_scale

[4] Chapter: Axiom of Resistance

[5] https://www.theatlantic.com/magazine/archive/2017/09/big-in-venezuela/534177/

[6] Chapter: Relay Fallacy

Given a perpetual positive pressure, transaction selection will eventually be reduced to one person's control. It is possible that this is already the case. The risk to Bitcoin is that one person is the sole defense[1] of utility, making successful co-option inevitable. This risk cannot be mitigated[2] by the economy.

Pooling pressure is a Bitcoin analogy to the United States Federal Reserve[3] system. The system was designed[4] to facilitate tax through debasement[5] of a market money. It offered state support[6] for a monetary proxy[7] in trade for market money[8]. This combination was designed to create a pressure to collect market money at the central authority. Once this collection was sufficient the state did away with the pretense and simply seized[9] all remaining market money. All states have similar systems and cooperate[10] to defend them.

This does not imply that mining is adversarial to Bitcoin. Following the analogy, free banking[11] is not adversarial to gold. Mining is a necessary part of Bitcoin. Pooling represents risk, though pooling pressure is not created by miners but by flaws in Bitcoin itself.

Reference

[1] Chapter: Risk Sharing Principle
[2] Chapter: Balance of Power Fallacy
[3] https://www.federalreserve.gov
[4] Chapter: State Banking Principle
[5] https://en.wikipedia.org/wiki/Debasement
[6] https://en.wikipedia.org/wiki/Legal_tender
[7] https://en.wikipedia.org/wiki/Federal_Reserve_Note
[8] Chapter: Money Taxonomy
[9] https://en.wikipedia.org/wiki/Executive_Order_6102
[10] https://en.wikipedia.org/wiki/International_Monetary_Fund
[11] https://en.wikipedia.org/wiki/Free_banking

Proximity Premium Flaw

Latency is the time required for communication. Information moves at a speed not greater than the speed of light[1] and therefore latency cannot be eliminated.

Different distances between miners implies announcements will be known to some before others. While a miner remains unaware of an announcement he wastes capital grinding on a weak candidate. As more time passes it becomes exponentially less likely that the miner will be rewarded for the candidate. Miners therefore compete to see announcements before other miners, as this reduces opportunity cost[2].

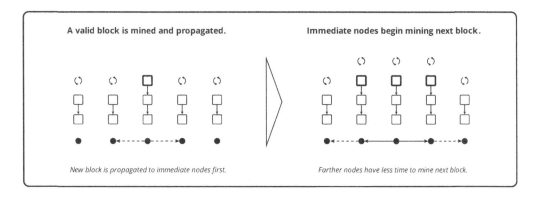

A valid block is mined and propagated.

Immediate nodes begin mining next block.

New block is propagated to immediate nodes first.

Farther nodes have less time to mine next block.

If we were to disperse miners with equal hash rate at equidistant points around the Earth they would experience the same average latency. Yet due to the financial benefit of reduced latency, they would tend to move closer to each other. Miners obtain a premium on returns for aggregating.

Reference

[1] https://en.wikipedia.org/wiki/Speed_of_light

[2] https://en.wikipedia.org/wiki/Opportunity_cost

This proximity-based pooling pressure[1] is a consequence of the linear block ordering required by consensus rules. **Bitcoin prescribes winner-take-all ordering, which produces disproportionate opportunity cost.** The variance discount[2] is the other pooling pressure caused by consensus.

The defense[3] that Bitcoin *intends* to raise is market defense against anti-market (state) forces. To do this hash power must be distributed broadly among people so that it becomes difficult to co-opt. However pooling pressures inherent in the consensus work against this objective. As such the characteristic is termed a flaw, though no way to eliminate the flaw has been discovered.

Reference

[1] Chapter: Pooling Pressure Risk
[2] Chapter: Variance Discount Flaw
[3] Chapter: Axiom of Resistance

Relay Fallacy

The peer-to-peer network disseminates blocks and unconfirmed transactions. The protocol itself allows nodes to protect against denial of service. Consequently this communication requires no identity. This protection is how the network avoids the need for permission to participate.

However this protection comes at a cost in terms of announcement latency, and because of the advantage to proximity, lower latency translates into higher apparent hash power. Therefore miners compete for reduced latency. One way to reduce latency is pooling, another is to use a more efficient dissemination network. Given that pooling surrenders power to the operator, presumably the latter option is preferable.

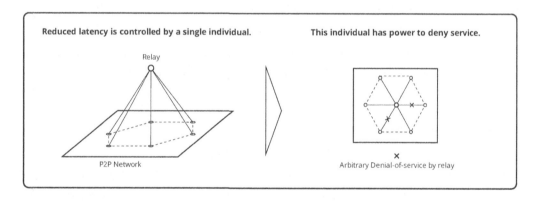

One way to improve dissemination is to *optimize* the peer-to-peer network. The other is to join a distinct network, called a relay, that has lower latency due to elimination of denial-of-service protections, for example[1]:

Reference

[1] http://bitcoinfibre.org

> [T]he cmpctblock message format was designed to ensure it fits neatly into a UDP-FEC-based relay mechanism. The only difference is that we send it over UDP with FEC... This way, extra hops do not introduce more latency. Sadly, due to the nature of our FEC encoding, we cannot know if individual packets are a part of a legitimate, or any, block, and thus only enable this optimization between nodes run by the same group.
>
> *bitcoinfibre.org*

The relay accepts communication from a set of miners, over the peer-to-peer or other protocol. The relay consists of a set of machines under the control of the relayer. It communicates the announcements within its internal network[1] and eventually to the joined miners.

The important security observation is that communication within the relay is under the relayer's control. Due to the removal of denial-of-service protections central control is *necessary* to the scheme. The relayer can delay certain blocks based on miner, region, signal, non-payment, etc. A relayer sells reduced latency, and is therefore in the mining business. From a security standpoint it matters not if this service is offered for free. Miners may similarly offer grinders free reduced latency and variance.

Relays are aggregations of miners and miners are aggregations of grinders. The greater the hash power aggregation, the more profitable is the mine, as is the relay. One may consider that grinders are free to leave mines and miners are free to leave relays, and it is of course possible for a grinder to run his own mine and his own relay. But larger aggregations are more profitable, so leaving the largest relay or mine increases relative cost[2].

A theory holds that relays reduce pooling pressure. This is an error. **Any pooling reduction caused by a relay does not disappear but is transferred to the relay as a pooling increase.** Relay statistics are not typically presented alongside mining statistics,

Reference

[1] https://bitcoinmagazine.com/articles/blockstream-satellite-broadcasting-bitcoin-space
[2] Chapter: Zero Sum Property

masking the power transfer. This may lead people to believe that mining is less strongly-pooled than is the case.

Selfish Mining Fallacy

The term selfish mining refers to a mining *optimization*. However, one academic paper[1] frames the optimization as follows:

> Conventional wisdom asserts that the mining protocol is incentive-compatible and secure against colluding minority groups, that is, it incentivizes miners to follow the protocol as prescribed. We show that the Bitcoin mining protocol is not incentive-compatible.
>
> *Ittay Eyal and Emin Gün Sirer: Majority is not Enough*

This statement assumes a "prescribed Bitcoin mining protocol" that precludes withholding, which is a straw man[2]. Bitcoin consensus rules are necessarily silent on the timing of announcements.

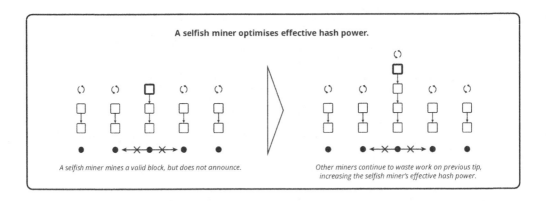

A selfish miner optimises effective hash power.

A selfish miner mines a valid block, but does not announce.

Other miners continue to waste work on previous tip, increasing the selfish miner's effective hash power.

> We present an attack with which colluding miners obtain a revenue larger than their fair share.

Reference

[1] https://www.cs.cornell.edu/~ie53/publications/btcProcFC.pdf

[2] https://en.wikipedia.org/wiki/Straw_man

This statement assumes a concept of "fair share" that is foreign to Bitcoin, another straw man. A miner is rewarded based on blocks that reach maturity, not as a proportion of actual hash rate.

These straw men are explicitly attributed to "conventional wisdom". In other words the paper uses them to show that the conventional wisdom is incorrect. However, the paper errs in unconditionally declaring that this supposedly *unfair violation of the protocol* constitutes an attack:

> This attack can have significant consequences for Bitcoin: Rational miners will prefer to join the selfish miners, and the colluding group will increase in size until it becomes a majority. At this point, the Bitcoin system ceases to be a decentralized currency.

This is the source of the fallacy. It is not an attack for conventional wisdom to be incorrect, it is an error in the presumed conventional wisdom. Selfish mining implies that Bitcoin exhibits latency-based pooling pressure[1], though this is a well-established flaw[2]. All pooling pressures tend to reduce the number of miners, exposing Bitcoin to attacks.

Optimizations are not attacks. Pooling increases the *opportunity* for attacks, but opportunity should not be conflated with action. The term "attack" implies theft. In fact, the Bitcoin whitepaper[3] uses the term only to describe double-spend attempts.

Reference

[1] Chapter: Pooling Pressure Risk

[2] Chapter: Proximity Premium Flaw

[3] https://bitcoin.org/bitcoin.pdf

Side Fee Fallacy

There is a theory that transaction fees paid externally represent an individual incentive that works counter to system security (incentive incompatible[1]). The theory holds that a merchant paying a miner "off-chain" to confirm the merchant's transactions prevents other merchants' transactions from being confirmed, or that it raises the cost of those confirmations, giving advantage to those who accept such fees.

One impact of such arrangements is that an average *historical* fee rate cannot be determined through chain analysis. The apparent rate would be lower than the market rate. This could of course lead spenders to underestimate a sufficient fee. However there is no aspect of Bitcoin that requires future fees to equal some average of past fees. Estimation necessarily compensates, such as by ignoring "free" transactions in full blocks or using standard deviation[2] to identify outliers. But fee estimation is just that, estimation. Actual fee levels are controlled by competition.

Another impact is that disparate relative fee levels can highlight certain transactions as being associated with such arrangements. This can contribute to taint of the merchant's transaction and/or the miner's coinbase. But given the arrangement is a choice made by the creators of these transactions, there is no privacy loss.

There is no impact on market fee rates or the ability of others to obtain confirmations. If the arrangement deviates from market rates then either the miner or the merchant is accepting an unnecessary loss. This is no different than the miner confirming transactions with below-market on-chain fees or the merchant overestimating on-chain fees, respectively. In any case there would be no harm to system security even if all fees were paid off chain.

Reference

[1] https://en.wikipedia.org/wiki/Incentive_compatibility
[2] https://en.wikipedia.org/wiki/Standard_deviation

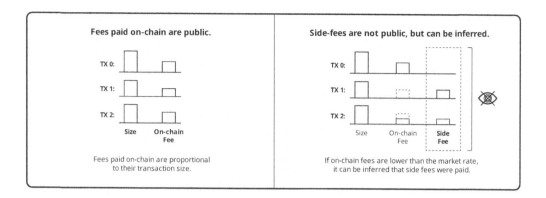

Fees paid on-chain are public.	Side-fees are not public, but can be inferred.

TX 0:
TX 1:
TX 2:

Size   On-chain
        Fee

Fees paid on-chain are proportional
to their transaction size.

TX 0:
TX 1:
TX 2:

Size   On-chain   Side
        Fee   Fee

If on-chain fees are lower than the market rate,
it can be inferred that side fees were paid.

Bitcoin provides a mechanism for on-chain fees so that a transaction can compensate *any* miner without the use of identity. It is a privacy-preserving convenience. **If miners and merchants prefer to weaken their own privacy by performing additional tasks, there is no basis to consider that undesirable.** This theory is therefore invalid.

Furthermore the merchant must accept a delayed confirmation time inversely proportional to the miner's hash power. The side-fee is offered at the market rate since the miner will incur an opportunity cost otherwise.

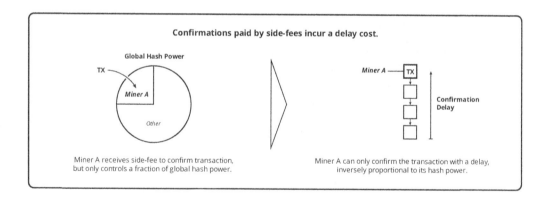

Confirmations paid by side-fees incur a delay cost.

Global Hash Power

TX

Miner A

Other

Miner A receives side-fee to confirm transaction,
but only controls a fraction of global hash power.

Miner A — TX

Confirmation
Delay

Miner A can only confirm the transaction with a delay,
inversely proportional to its hash power.

There is a related theory that side fee arrangements constitute a pooling pressure[1]. If fees paid are consistent with the market there can be no effect on pooling. Above market fees

Reference

[1] Chapter: Pooling Pressure Risk

are a state subsidy, as we must treat the subsidy as not economically rational. Below market fees are a tax, as we must treat the loss as involuntary. These are distortions just like any other state subsidy/tax and are therefore not unique to side fees. As such the existence of side fees does not create a new pooling pressure beyond what exists with on-chain fees, and the theory is therefore invalid.

Spam Misnomer

The term spam[1] in computing originally referred to excessive Usenet cross-posting and later became a synonym for unwanted broadcast email. While there is no clear distinction between wanted and unwanted email, the messages carry identity, are not fungible, and do not carry payment for processing by the recipient. Bitcoin transactions by comparison are necessarily anonymous[2], fungible and carry payment for processing.

While email spam detection is a subjective process, it is necessary due to the lack of payment for processing. This process is facilitated by identity and lack of fungibility. By contrast, due to anonymity and the fungibility objective, there is no test possible for transaction legitimacy, and due to payment there is no need for it. In other words **all valid transactions are equally legitimate**, and this does not subject nodes to denial of service. A proper name for a transaction with a low fee is "low fee transaction."

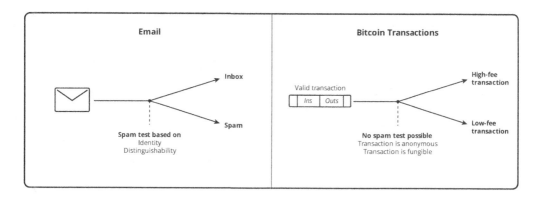

High volume submission of redundant transactions is a typical denial of service problem that is independent of the transaction fee and can be carried out by any person, not limited to the spender. Non-redundant transactions that incorporate mutually-

Reference

[1] https://en.m.wikipedia.org/wiki/History_of_email_spam
[2] Chapter: Risk Sharing Principle

conflicting spends are not a denial of service risk, since they are either rejected as invalid or accepted due to a sufficient fee increment.

Variance Discount Flaw

Variance is the varying frequency of achieving a reward. Variance is inherent to the probabilistic nature of mining and cannot be eliminated.

As a matter of consensus, different hash power among miners implies rewards will be earned by some more frequently than others. With 10% hash rate one might expect to be rewarded 10 times more frequently than with 1%. Actual results are unpredictable and can vary significantly. But it is sufficient here in both cases to assume proportionality. In this example one miner receives a reward every 100 minutes and the other every 1000 minutes. Assuming identical rewards per block, the magnitude of the reward is also proportional to hash power.

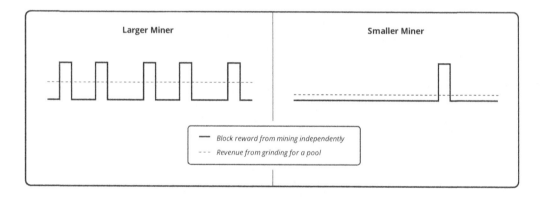

Consider then that a tiny miner might have to wait years before any reward. There is also the possibility that a mine is misconfigured and can never succeed. Despite being rewarded proportionally, a smaller miner is faced with a deficiency in relation to the larger miner. It must improve cash flow[1] to receive a fraction of the reward more frequently. For these reasons miners discount returns for variance. Smaller miners will convert their mines to grinds and pay an aggregating miner for reduced variance.

Reference

[1] https://en.wikipedia.org/wiki/Operating_cash_flow

Avoiding this aggregation is the rationale behind P2Pool[1], but because distributed variance reduction is less efficient, pooling dominates.

This variance-based pooling pressure[2] is a consequence of singular difficulty as required by consensus rules. **Small miners must compete at high difficulty despite low hash power, which magnifies inherent variance.** The proximity premium[3] is the other pooling pressure caused by consensus.

The defense[4] that Bitcoin *intends* to raise is market defense against anti-market (state) forces. To do this hash power must be distributed broadly among people so that it becomes difficult to co-opt. However pooling pressures inherent in the consensus work against this objective. As such the characteristic is termed a flaw, though no way to eliminate the flaw has been discovered.

Reference

[1] https://en.bitcoin.it/wiki/P2Pool
[2] Chapter: Pooling Pressure Risk
[3] Chapter: Proximity Premium Flaw
[4] Chapter: Axiom of Resistance

Zero Sum Property

Bitcoin mining is a zero sum game[1]. On average the chain grows by one block every 10 minutes, with the full reward controlled by its miner. Miners compete to achieve this reward and will, apart from pooling pressures[2], each average a number of rewards proportional to hash rate. The difference between a miner's cost and this reward over time is the interest on capital invested in the mine.

There are two aspects of the zero sum property:

- For the time period between organizations one miner earns a reward and all other miners earn no reward. Neither price, hash rate, difficulty, inflation, fees, nor anything else has any effect on this property.

- The magnitude of rewards, in either coin units or exchange price, has no effect on the rate of return on capital.

Idealized Bitcoin mining is a closed system[3]. Return on capital varies relative to other mines, due to the proximity premium[4] and variance discount[5] protocol flaws, as well as economies of scale[6] and operator efficiency. **Yet because these only impact the relative cost of hash power, the proportionality of return rates is affected, not overall returns.**

Actual Bitcoin is not a closed system. The market and anti-market pooling pressures of variation and distortion (respectively) are external. Fundamentally Bitcoin exists to defend markets, necessarily pitting distortion against variation (or lack thereof).

Reference

[1] https://en.wikipedia.org/wiki/Zero-sum_game
[2] Chapter: Pooling Pressure Risk
[3] https://en.wikipedia.org/wiki/Closed_system
[4] Chapter: Proximity Premium Flaw
[5] Chapter: Variance Discount Flaw
[6] https://en.wikipedia.org/wiki/Economies_of_scale

When a distortion is applied to a miner in this zero sum system, all other miners are affected. For example, a subsidy[1] (not to be confused with a consensus subsidy) to one miner acts as a tax on all others, and a tax on one miner acts as a subsidy to all others. The subsidized miner operates at a lower cost for the same hash rate, or has a higher effective hash rate (i.e. hash power) for the same cost. The taxed miner operates at a higher cost for the same hash rate, or has a lower effective hash rate for the same cost.

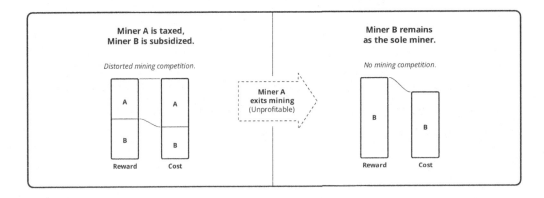

A subsidizer expects no return on capital, otherwise he/she would be considered an investor. Investment is a market force whereby the miner pays a market price for capital. With a higher effective rate of return the subsidized miner attracts more capital than other miners, continuing to expand hash power until there is a majority hash power miner. The subsidizer's objective is ultimately *control* over the subsidized mine.

A tax on mining has the effect of moving hash power to untaxed mines, beyond the reach of the taxing authority, as capital seeks market returns. If applied broadly, this can give the authority control through its own mining operation. In other words, the authority can suppress competition. This can also be accomplished through a 100% tax, whereby the authority co-opts mines. The effect is the same, the taxed miner is put out of business, and the proceeds of the tax are applied to control.

Reference

[1] https://en.wikipedia.org/wiki/Subsidy

The consequences of zero sum mining with inherent pooling pressure are explored in Threat Level Paradox[1].

Reference

[1] Chapter: Threat Level Paradox

ALTERNATIVES

Bitcoin Labels

Bitcoin has since its inception defied clear definition[1]. This is a consequence of the heavily overloaded use of the term. The term was coined by Satoshi in Bitcoin: A Peer-to-Peer Electronic Cash System[2], as a label for the essential concepts. It was later used also for the prototype implementation, a chain (history) of transaction confirmation, a set of consensus rules that constrain a chain, a unit of the coin, and a vaguely-bounded community of people.

While there is only one set of concepts, each of the other contexts has any number of possible variations consistent with them. There are many implementations (of the prototype and otherwise), consensus rules have deviated (in the prototype and in other implementations), history is dynamic and arbitrary (even the prototype-encoded genesis block could have been different without consequence), and each coin manifests an independent set of units and is supported by its own set of adherents.

For these reasons Bitcoin is used herein as a label for Cryptodynamic Principles[3]. Implementations are referred to by their brands[4], such as "Bitcoin Core"[5] or "Libbitcoin"[6]; chains are referred to by the trading symbols in common use, such as "BTC" and "LTC"; consensus rules for a given chain are referred to in the context of the trading symbol, such as "LTC consensus rules"; a unit of coin is referred to in the lower case of the trading symbol, such as "btc" or "ltc" (a refinement of the ambiguous convention of using lower

Reference

[1] http://gavinandresen.ninja/a-definition-of-bitcoin
[2] https://bitcoin.org/bitcoin.pdf
[3] Chapter: Cryptodynamic Principles
[4] Chapter: Brand Arrogation
[5] https://bitcoin.org/en/bitcoin-core
[6] https://libbitcoin.info

case "bitcoin" to refer to a unit of "BTC"); and communities are referred to as either "Bitcoin community" (generally) or "BTC community" (specifically).

While maximalists1 may reject the use "Bitcoin" as a conceptual label, associating it instead with a history, **the term was coined in relation to a set of principles and continues to apply to them.** Furthermore there are multiple instances of independent chains that adhere to those principles, making the history-based label ambiguous. Due to this ambiguity people have naturally adopted the convention of referring to histories unambiguously by way of trading symbols.

Reference

[1] Chapter: Maximalism Definition

Blockchain Fallacy

There is a theory that property ownership can be secured by immutable claim-keeping, both against claim loss and Custodial Risk[1].

Given that a claim is not itself the property, control of the property rests with the custodian against whom the claim is made. A custodian has the ability to surrender or retain the property and is therefore a trusted third party[2]. Abrogation of a claim by its custodian is always mitigated by custodian signature, cryptographic or otherwise, with enforcement of the claim left to its holder.

The theory asserts that immutable claim-keeping provides security against loss of the claim by its owner, as nobody else would have an interest in the loss. However, in order to redeem the claim its owner must produce proof of ownership to the custodian. This requires that the owner not lose the secret that proves this ownership. As such the security of the claim against loss is not mitigated at all, it merely changes form. The theory is therefore invalid on the basis of loss prevention.

Storing a strong reference to the claim can reduce the size, and therefore cost, of its immutable storage. The claim may be in the form of a human or machine contract, and referenced as a one way hash[3]. In either case the validation and execution of the contract is required for property transfer by the custodian. Therefore a referenced contract claim compounds loss risk with additional data, the contract.

Reference

[1] Chapter: Custodial Risk Principle
[2] https://en.wikipedia.org/wiki/Trusted_third_party
[3] https://en.wikipedia.org/wiki/Cryptographic_hash_function

As shown in Risk Sharing Principle[1], people are always the basis of security. People may act collectively to protect the immutability of a money, and therefore any claim data associated with control of the money.

However, a custodian is a trusted third party. Immutable claims do not in any way mitigate direct attacks against, or by, a custodian. Where the custodian is the state or is subject to its control, the claim offers no security[2] against the substitution of state authority in place of proven ownership of any claim. The theory is therefore also invalid on the basis of custodial failure.

Bitcoin as a money[3] is non-custodial. Its units do not represent an asset held by a trusted third party. The money is traded directly between customer and merchant. In this sense *all merchants* are custodians of Bitcoin's value. **The blockchain fallacy arises from a misconception of the Bitcoin security model, attributing security to its technology as opposed to its distribution of merchants.** The term "blockchain technology" reinforces this error, implying that it is primarily the structure of Bitcoin's data that secures it.

Reference

[1] Chapter: Risk Sharing Principle

[2] https://en.m.wikipedia.org/wiki/Executive_Order_6102

[3] Chapter: Money Taxonomy

Brand Arrogation

Bitcoin is a set of essential concepts[1], not a chain. No person can control the concepts. People will use it to describe one or more chains and splits as they evolve. This happens with all monies[2], including gold and oil which trade at different purities and qualities.

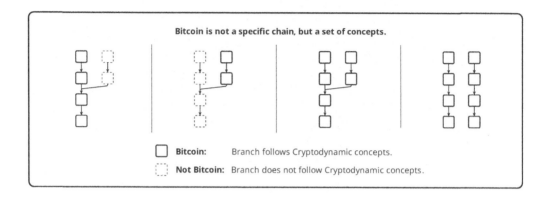

Bitcoin is not a specific chain, but a set of concepts.

☐ **Bitcoin:** Branch follows Cryptodynamic concepts.
⬚ **Not Bitcoin:** Branch does not follow Cryptodynamic concepts.

This is consistent with the declaration of Bitcoin[3], as it binds a set of concepts, not a set of rules, protocols, or implementations. **People with capital invested have an inherent desire for brand association, but there is no such thing as a "legitimate" claim to it.**

Reference

[1] Chapter: Cryptodynamic Principles
[2] Chapter: Money Taxonomy
[3] https://bitcoin.org/bitcoin.pdf

Consolidation Principle

The need to exchange from one coin in order to trade with merchants of another is a cost. This cost must be non-zero even if automated, as it must consume space and/or time. As such one coin is always "better" (higher utility) than two, to the extent that the resulting coin does not become fee bound as implied by the utility threshold[1].

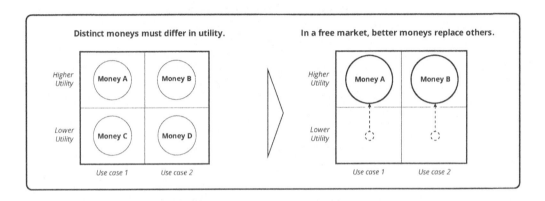

We can reasonably assume that two distinct monies[2] cannot perpetually have identical utility. Thiers' Law[3] discusses the consequences of better money in the absence of state controls. From this we necessarily conclude that **the better of the two monies will eventually replace the other** in the absence of state controls. As this occurs utility accrues to the surviving coin in the reverse of the manner detailed in Fragmentation Principle[4].

Reference

[1] Chapter: Utility Threshold Property

[2] Chapter: Money Taxonomy

[3] https://en.wikipedia.org/wiki/Gresham%27s_law#Reverse_of_Gresham's_law_(Thiers'_law)

[4] Chapter: Fragmentation Principle

This does not imply that new coins cannot be created or exist over a significant amount of time. It implies that there is a market pressure toward a single coin. A better money in one situation may not be a better or even useful money in another.

For example, gold is not a useful money for electronic transfer and bitcoin is not very useful without a network. One money replaces another in the scenarios for which the former is better.

Dumping Fallacy

There is a theory that selling units from one side of a split coin for units of the other reduces the relative utility of the "sold" coin. However each party is selling (and buying). As a trade the action is symmetrical and therefore the theory is invalid.

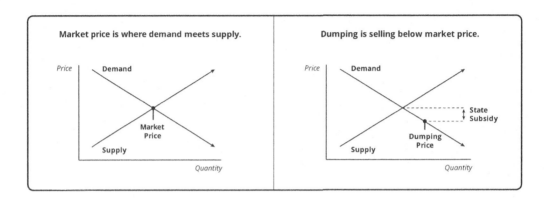

There is a related theory that exchanging units from one side of a split coin constitutes dumping[1] of that coin, which reduces its utility. **The theory simply misrepresents the concept of dumping.** Dumping is state subsidy[2] (not to be confused with Bitcoin subsidy) of a product sold in another state. It is a levy on the taxpayers of the subsidizing state, typically applied to establish market share for the product. In the case where demand is elastic[3], the subsidy increases sales volume for the product by reducing price relative to the otherwise market price. The lower price increases demand, by capturing buyers with lower marginal utility[4] for the product, until the market clears. In contrast to dumping, trading at market price doesn't reduce price because it is not subsidized.

Reference

[1] https://en.m.wikipedia.org/wiki/Dumping_(pricing_policy)

[2] https://en.m.wikipedia.org/wiki/Subsidyhttps://en.m.wikipedia.org/wiki/Subsidy

[3] https://en.m.wikipedia.org/wiki/Price_elasticity_of_demand

[4] https://en.wikipedia.org/wiki/Marginal_utility

Finally, there is a related theory that reduction of hoarding[1] generally reduces exchange prices of the hoarded property. This is true[2], however a transfer is not a reduction to hoarding levels unless the buyer of the hoarded property subsequently hoards it less than the seller. It is an error to assume this is the case.

Reference

[1] https://en.m.wikipedia.org/wiki/Hoarding_(economics)
[2] https://mises.org/blog/problem-hoarding

Fragmentation Principle

The utility of a money[1] derives directly from its ability to facilitate trade, in contrast to barter[2]. If it is not accepted by *any* merchant then objectively it has no monetary usefulness. The more goods and services[3] (including consideration of location) that can be purchased with a money at any given time, the more likely it is that the money represents greater utility to any given person.

A split implies that zero or more merchants have stopped accepting the original coin and that zero or more have started accepting the split coin. A "clean" split is a hypothetical scenario in which there is no overlap in merchant acceptance of the two coins, and no change in the set of merchants. A clean split produces two economies from the original set of merchants.

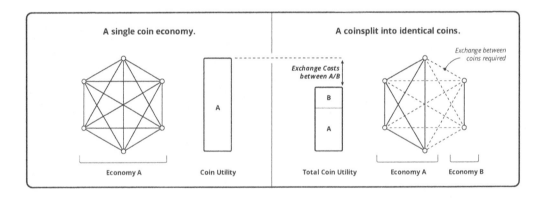

If we assume that the coins are identical apart from the fact of the split, the Consolidation Principle[4] implies that the utility of the combined coins is the same as the utility of the original less the exchange cost. The scenario can be expanded to include merchant

Reference

[1] Chapter: Money Taxonomy
[2] https://en.wikipedia.org/wiki/Barter
[3] https://en.wikipedia.org/wiki/Goods_and_services
[4] Chapter: Consolidation Principle

overlap. This has no effect on coin utility, as it only shifts the incidence of the exchange cost from buyer to seller.

An increase or decrease in the number of merchants accepting either of the coins is a net gain or loss of combined utility respectively, as it implies the removal or addition of a currency exchange cost. In other words the effect is proportional to each of the coins in the split. This factor relates to the particulars of a given split, not to splitting in general.

Therefore a split produces both a shift and reduction of utility, in proportion to the relative sizes of the resulting economies. The Network Effect Fallacy[1] explains why the reduction is not quadratic in nature, as sometimes assumed.

While it may appear that in the shift someone has "taken" value from the original coin, that value has actually "left" to form the split coin. In other words merchants are masters of the value that they provide to a money. Owners have independent influence over purchasing power, based on their level of hoarding[2]. However this affects unit price, not utility.

Upon the split an original unit becomes two units, each with decreased and proportional utility in relation to the original. With bidirectional mandatory replay protection[3] each can be spent at no additional cost. Otherwise the need for self-protection discounts[4] units of the unprotected chain(s).

This analysis is applicable to new coins as well. The difference in the case of a new coin is that original (other) coin units are not spendable on the new chain. As such the new coin is faced with the difficulty of allocating units, which requires work and therefore time.

Reference

[1] Chapter: Network Effect Fallacy
[2] Chapter: Dumping Fallacy
[3] Chapter: Replay Protection Fallacy
[4] https://en.m.wikipedia.org/wiki/Net_present_value

Splits bootstrap[1] this process by subdividing the utility of an existing chain, to the extent its merchants are willing to do so.

Reference

[1] https://en.wikipedia.org/wiki/Bootstrapping

Alternatives

Genetic Purity Fallacy

There is a theory that a coin is strongest when all validation is performed by a common implementation. According to this theory the complexity of consensus rule implementation implies a likelihood that multiple implementations will diverge, resulting an inadvertent chain split. The split implies financial loss by people on the weaker side. In addition to divergence, a single implementation risks a global stall of the network. The threat of financial loss implies lower utility and therefore system security.

Based on the presumption of high complexity, each update to the "one true client" produces the same likelihood of divergence. Similarly, dependency on external independently updated libraries has the same effect. In other words *it is not possible for there to be just one implementation*. In the case of the initial Bitcoin implementation both upgrade of the client[1] and upgrade of an external dependency[2] have resulted in unintended chain splits and material financial loss[3]. Additionally, zero-day[4] flaws in this implementation have been published without notice[5] and could have produced a global stall.

A single implementation would produce a weakness directly analogous to that of a living species with genetic uniformity. In the case of a single implementation, both internal and external updates penetrate the economy quickly and deeply. The financial impact of a split is therefore more significant than that caused by a less widely deployed implementation. In a scenario where ten implementations each supporting an even

Reference

[1] https://github.com/bitcoin/bips/blob/master/bip-0050.mediawiki

[2] https://github.com/bitcoin/bips/blob/master/bip-0066.mediawiki

[3] https://cointelegraph.com/news/miners-lost-over-50000-from-the-bitcoin-hardfork-last-weekend

[4] https://en.wikipedia.org/wiki/Zero-day_(computing)

[5] https://www.reddit.com/r/btc/comments/6z827o/chris_jeffrey_jj_discloses_bitcoin_attack_vector/

fraction of the economy there would be risk to at most 10% of the economy for any given update, whereas the update of a single universally deployed implementation reaches the maximum split risk of 50%. The theory is therefore not only invalid but expresses the opposite of actual behavior.

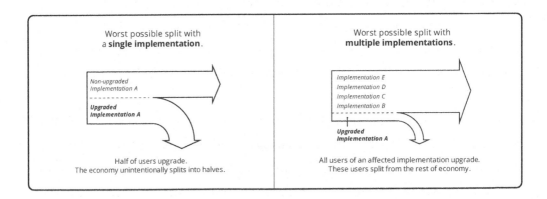

Alternatives

Hybrid Mining Fallacy

There is a theory that a combination of proof-of-work (PoW) and proof-of-stake (PoS) mining offers a higher level of system security than PoW. The theory implies that a majority of coin owners can mitigate "misbehavior" by PoW miners.

In the absence of a majority hash power miner, there is nothing to mitigate. Therefore the theory is premised on increasing the cost of a censorship regime. This rests on the unsupportable assumption that PoW miners are not also PoS miners.

The cost of hybrid mining is the combined costs of work and staking, inclusive of capital cost. The return on mining investment necessarily equates to capital cost, as a consequence of competition. As mining is profitable, capital cost does not contribute to security. **Achieving majority stake is no more costly than achieving majority hash power.** The theory is therefore invalid.

Given a model whereby a majority stakeholder can prevent confirmation of otherwise valid PoW blocks, once a majority is achieved the censor cannot be unseated[1]. Such a system is fundamentally a PoS coin, lacking censorship resistance[2], with the PoW aspect providing no additional security.

Reference

[1] Chapter: Proof of Stake Fallacy
[2] Chapter: Censorship Resistance Property

Maximalism Definition

Maximalism is a public relations effort to discourage the formation of substitutes for a given coin. To the extent this is successful it may benefit existing owners by restricting supply and subsequently elevating price. However as people fail to find close substitutes[1], activity moves to more distant ones. In the case of electronic payments this is generally state money.

Maximalism is distinct from shitcoin awareness in that it is characterized by promotion of one Bitcoin over all others. Proponents often express the contradictory theory that no other coin could be competitive with their preferred coin. If this were the case there would be no reason to advocate for a single coin.

Reference

[1] Chapter: Substitution Principle

Network Effect Fallacy

There is a theory that the utility created by an economy varies with the square of the number of its merchants, assuming each merchant offers the same value of goods or services for sale in the one coin. The theory is an application of Metcalfe's Law[1].

This implies that an even split of the economy reduces combined utility by half. For example, if 20 merchants has utility 400 then 2 networks of 10 of these merchants has utility 200.

However, the ability to exchange any units of one coin for the other collapses the utility of the two economies into a hybrid economy. Due to the conversion cost[2] **the hybrid coin has lower utility than would a single, but this cannot be comparable to loss of one of the two entirely unless the conversion cost is unbounded.** The theory is therefore invalid.

Reference

[1] https://en.wikipedia.org/wiki/Metcalfe%27s_law
[2] Chapter: Consolidation Principle

Proof of Cost Fallacy

In a competitive (free) market, Bitcoin mining consumes in cost to the miner what it creates in value to the miner, both in the issuance of new units and in the service of confirmation. This is the case whether a mined block reward reflects the miner's full return or otherwise.

The amount of computation performed in mining is probabilistically reflected in the block difficulty. This computation is referred to as work. A valid block header is probabilistic proof that this work was performed. This is the basis of the term "proof of work".

The amount of energy consumed in block production is not provable, either specifically or probabilistically. Energy efficiency varies. A block header does not reflect "proof of energy" consumed. Such claims are approximations.

A miner's return on block production is not fully reflected by the block. The mining of one's own transactions implies fees not necessarily reflected in the block, as do side fees[1] generally. A miner may introduce transactions with arbitrarily high or low fees. The block reward does not represent a "proof of reward". Such claims are assumptions.

In a free market, the return on mining is the value of its reward, whether or not the amount is reflected in the block, and the fees earned are determined by demand to transact. This is a consequence of competition. So in this case it is correct to consider a valid block header to be "proof of cost", however the amount of the cost remains unknown. All that is knowable is that the miner earned a market rate of return on capital.

Reference

[1] Chapter: Side Fee Fallacy

However, in the case of state monopoly[1], price is not controlled by competition. A monopoly may charge any price that the market will bear. The enforcement cost of monopoly is paid by the taxpayer. The price premium is another tax, paid by the consumer. The value of the tax is transferred to the monopoly.

In the case of state-sponsored Bitcoin censorship, both enforcement and price (fee) premium exist as taxes in the manner of monopoly. The fee level may exceed a market rate, and its enforcement is subsidized by taxes. Monopoly mining can produce seigniorage[2] just as any monopoly money. The block header continues to provide a proof of work, but no longer provides a proof of market cost.

In the same manner, the existence of a valid unit of monopoly money[3] provides sufficient proof of a real production cost, but provides no proof that the issuer did not earn a monopoly premium on this cost. There is a theory that Bitcoin's production cost is "unforgeable", where seigniorage of state money represents "cost forgery". As has been shown, **Bitcoin is also subject to seigniorage**, invalidating the theory.

All goods have real production cost. Monopoly exists to raise price above cost. While Bitcoin is censorship resistant[4], the effectiveness of resistance is not guaranteed[5].

Reference

[1] https://mises.org/library/man-economy-and-state-power-and-market/html/pp/1054
[2] https://en.wikipedia.org/wiki/Seigniorage
[3] Chapter: Money Taxonomy
[4] Chapter: Censorship Resistance Property
[5] Chapter: Axiom of Resistance

Proof of Memory Façade

It has been proposed[1] that a proof-of-memory (PoM) can replace some fraction of the proof-of-work (PoW) energy cost with hardware, even relying on existing memory devices. As shown in Energy Waste Fallacy[2], a constant level of security requires a constant ongoing expenditure. Therefore such a system would require a comparable level of hardware consumption to offset any reduction in energy cost. **In other words total energy consumption cannot be reduced, it can only be transferred to hardware manufacture, operation and disposal.**

In December 2017 the estimated annualized cost of energy consumed in Bitcoin mining was $1,628,000,000, based on the approximations of 32.56 terawatt hours consumed at an average $.05 per kilowatt hour energy cost. Contemporaneously this cost level equates to the consumption of 32,560,000 terabyte drives at an average price of $50 per drive. Utilization of existing underutilized memory reduces the unit cost and therefore comparably increases the size requirement.

It is worth considering the economic behavior of a theoretical system in which PoM is determined by an existing (cost free) fixed pool of memory with no expiration or operational costs. As the cost of mining is zero, rewards flow at no expense in proportion to memory (assuming no pooling pressures[3]). Any increase in average fee increases this reward for memory. Capital invested is zero and therefore rate of interest is perpetually infinite. Despite unbounded incentive, the assumption of zero expansion precludes competition. But since the proof is externalized, competition cannot actually be restricted. In an actual system hardware manufacture expands perpetually for a given fee level, and this expansion accelerates with fee level increases.

Reference

[1] https://eprint.iacr.org/2017/893.pdf
[2] Chapter: Energy Waste Fallacy
[3] Chapter: Pooling Pressure Risk

Proof-of-memory is equal to proof-of-work in terms of resource consumption and there is no reason to assume a reduced energy component of that cost. The hardware acts as a proof battery, representing energy provably consumed in its manufacture. This is a façade analogous to the "zero emission" battery-powered car.

Proof of Stake Fallacy

Confirmation security requires a person of authority to order transactions. Bitcoin periodically assigns this authority to the miner who produces the greatest proof of work. All forms of work necessarily[1] reduce to energy consumption[2]. It is essential[3] that such proof be independent of the chain history. We can refer to this as "external" proof.

The only other source of ordering authority is therefore dependent upon chain history, which we can refer to as "internal". There is a theory that such proof-of-stake (PoS) constitutes a comparable alternative to proof-of-work (PoW) in terms of confirmation security. It is true that both PoS and PoW delegate control over transaction ordering to a person in control of the largest pool of certain capital.

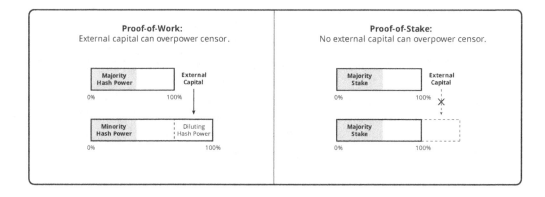

The distinction is in the deployability of the capital. PoW excludes capital that cannot be converted to work, while PoS excludes capital that cannot acquire units of the coin. This difference has a material consequence for security.

Reference

[1] Chapter: Proof of Memory Façade
[2] Chapter: Energy Waste Fallacy
[3] Chapter: Censorship Resistance Property

In Other Means Principle[1] it is shown that censorship resistance depends on people paying miners to overpower the censor. **Overcoming censorship is not possible in a PoS system, as the censor has acquired majority stake and cannot be unseated.** As such PoS systems are not censorship-resistant and the theory is therefore invalid.

Reference

[1] Chapter: Other Means Principle

Replay Protection Fallacy

There is a theory that replay protection applied in a split chain increases the relative utility of the original chain. Replay protection is a rule designed relative to another chain and with a directional behavior. The protection makes transactions of the protected chain invalid on the other.

Even without protection it is possible for an owner to spend in a manner that prevents replay in one direction or the other, though there is a fee and/or complexity cost in doing so. A split may reduce, but not eliminate, this cost in one or both directions by activating rules that spends can selectively utilize. This is called opt-in, in contrast to mandatory, replay protection. Opt-in replay protection reduces but does not eliminate the cost whereas mandatory protection can eliminate the cost.

The replay of a spend onto another chain is non-dilutive[1]. The common output can be spent on either chain with or without replay. **The only distinction provided by protection is that spends can always be distinct on each chain with no extra cost to the spender.** The supply in each chain remains unaffected by protection.

It is a curious misperception that one chain can somehow absorb the transactions of another in a split. All outputs of the common segment remain spendable on both chains. Replay protection only reduces the cost of spending them on the protected chain.

One might assume that the lack of protection makes an owner less likely to spend on the unprotected chain, thereby limiting supply and increasing exchange price. However this assumes demand is unaffected by what amounts to an increase in trading cost. If the

Reference

[1] https://en.m.wikipedia.org/wiki/Stock_dilution

Alternatives

owner is not trading because of an increased cost in doing so, then the utility of the coin is not increased but decreased.

The self-protection cost amounts to a one-time demurrage[1] that persists until protection is applied to unprotected units, intentionally or otherwise. This cost is a discount[2] to the utility of an unprotected chain in relation to the hypothetical same chain with protection. This implies *greater* utility of a protected chain relative to the unprotected chain against which it is split than would otherwise be the case. Therefore the theory is invalid.

Reference

[1] https://en.m.wikipedia.org/wiki/Demurrage
[2] https://en.m.wikipedia.org/wiki/Net_present_value

Shitcoin Definition

A shitcoin is any system that is not cryptodynamically secure[1] yet purports to capture the value proposition[2] of Bitcoin.

Shitcoins are presumed to be scams, though it remains possible for proponents be to well-intentioned yet ignorant of cryptodynamic principles. By way of example, proof-of-stake[3] technologies are shitcoins.

While there may be implementations of Bitcoin that are more secure than others, these are matters of degree. No Bitcoin can be shown to be absolutely secure[4]. As such the term is not reasonably applied to any Bitcoin. By way of example, proof-of-memory[5] technologies may not be shitcoins (despite failure to achieve central objectives).

Reference

[1] Chapter: Cryptodynamic Principles
[2] Chapter: Value Proposition
[3] Chapter: Proof of Stake Fallacy
[4] Chapter: Axiom of Resistance
[5] Chapter: Proof of Memory Façade

Split Credit Expansion Fallacy

There is a theory that the increase of monetary units, as in the case of a split or new coin, creates credit. This is an error that is presumably a consequence of assuming that credit expansion[1] driven by state monetary expansion is a market force. This assumption fails to consider that market money[2] cannot produce seigniorage[3].

Seigniorage is a tax. The created monetary units do not represent new capital but instead the dilution of existing units by the state, transferring ownership of the capital that they represent to the sovereign. As this capital is put to use in the subsidy of lending by the state banking[4] cartel, as discounted money[5] and insurance[6], the cost of capital to the bank's customers is reduced.

This so-called credit expansion is not simply the result of fractional banking as a market force, it is the consequence of the state favoring debtors at the expense of savers. In a free market of banking, banks are simply *investment funds*. Investors on average obtain a market return on capital and suffer the risk of doing so. In state banking, risk, and therefore capital, are rearranged according to political objectives.

Market credit expansion is an increase in the lending of capital, as opposed to its hoarding. Increased rates of lending are a consequence of reduced time preference[7], and reduce the cost of capital. It is impossible to show that creation of a split or new coin (or

Reference

[1] Chapter: Credit Expansion Fallacy
[2] Chapter: Money Taxonomy
[3] https://en.wikipedia.org/wiki/Seigniorage
[4] Chapter: State Banking Principle
[5] https://www.frbdiscountwindow.org
[6] https://www.fdic.gov/resources/deposit-insurance
[7] https://en.wikipedia.org/wiki/Time_preference

anything else) reduces time preference. As such it is an error to assume that these creations either increase the availability of capital or reduce its cost.

Split Speculator Dilemma

In the wake of a split an original coin owner is faced with the choice of retaining or selling units of the original and split chains.

As discussed in Dumping Fallacy[1] there is no way to discourage the existence of one chain or the other by exchanging or hoarding[2] units of either. Therefore we consider this choice to be strictly a question of how to maximize the value of existing holdings following a split.

Given a position before the split, an owner is impacted by the increased cost of unit conversion, and replay protection[3] as applicable. These are unavoidable future trading costs that reduce the net present value[4] of the units. Therefore these factors are not relevant to the question.

The remaining considerations *assume* that the combined coins will increase in price over the contemplated period of time.

Under the assumptions of the Consolidation Principle[5] two similar coins will eventually consolidate, reducing to zero the value of one of them over time. If one happens to know which this will be, it is rational to sell it and buy the other. However, given that one may *not* know which coin will survive, there is a chance that the trade would sell the coin that succeeds for the one that fails, sacrificing *all* value in the original units. **With no knowledge of the future, selling all or part of one for the other increases the potential**

Reference

[1] Chapter: Dumping Fallacy
[2] https://en.m.wikipedia.org/wiki/Hoarding_(economics)
[3] Chapter: Replay Protection Fallacy
[4] https://en.m.wikipedia.org/wiki/Net_present_value
[5] Chapter: Consolidation Principle

reward in proportion to the increased risk. As such it is equally rational to hoard both, which preserves the assumptions that existed prior to the split.

Finally it should be emphasized that both chains could fail, with value consolidating to an independent chain, commodity, or *state* money. This topic intends only to provide a rational decision framework based on assumptions that may not come to pass.

ECONOMICS

Credit Expansion Fallacy

Credit expansion is the multiplication of credit against money[1], resulting from lending. When a loan is issued the lender and borrower both appear to hold the same money. Due to the apparent inflationary[2] nature of credit expansion, it is commonly treated as an adverse effect on people holding the money. Because banks are the most visible lenders this effect is often attributed to banking itself. There is a theory that Bitcoin can eliminate the effects of fractional banking[3] and thereby eliminate credit expansion.

Saving encompasses hoarding and investing. Hoarding implies ongoing depreciation[4], which is actual consumption. Investing is lending to production, and implies no depreciation as products must exist before they can depreciate. Investment includes both debt and equity contracts as the distinction is strictly financial, having no economic significance[5].

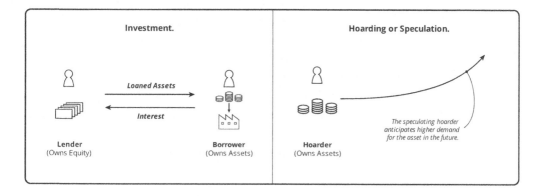

Reference

[1] Chapter: Money Taxonomy

[2] https://en.wikipedia.org/wiki/Monetary_inflation

[3] https://en.m.wikipedia.org/wiki/Fractional-reserve_banking

[4] Chapter: Depreciation Principle

[5] https://mises.org/library/man-economy-and-state-power-and-market/html/p/996

The distinction between hoarding and investment is essential to the understanding of credit expansion. Hoarded money is under the control of its owner, as if in a vault, buried in the back yard, or stuffed in a mattress.

This is inherent in the meaning of ownership. The lender of money is not the owner of the money, even though a loan is considered savings.

A lender requires liquidity to operate, and as such must hoard a certain fraction of savings. When a loan is created the borrower owns the amount lent. The borrower also requires liquidity, and so hoards a certain fraction of the loan. Any remainder of the loan is necessarily invested. This implies that the borrower has become a lender. The process continues until all capital that exists is hoarded.

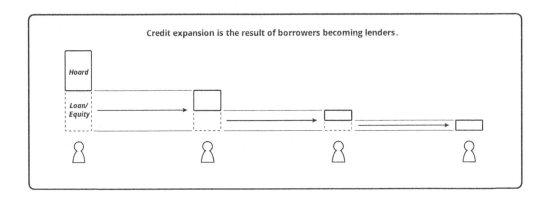

The amount hoarded is sometimes referred to as the owner's "reserve", but properly it is the owner's hoard, a fraction of that owner's total savings. This use of the word reserve should not be confused with its use in the state money context of reserve currency[1] (i.e. foreign exchange reserves[2]). The term "fractional reserve banking" is a reference to the ratio of a bank's hoard to its issued credit (money accounts).

Reference

[1] Chapter: Reserve Currency Fallacy

[2] https://en.wikipedia.org/wiki/Foreign-exchange_reserves

The total amount of U.S. Dollars in circulation[1] is referred to as "M0". This includes all tangible currency ("vault cash") plus intangible bank balances in Federal Reserve accounts. These two forms are considered interchangeable obligations of the Fed[2]. The intangible obligations are money that is accounted for but not yet printed[3]. As reported by the Fed[4], the total of U.S. Dollars is:

Dollars	Amount (2019)
Tangible	$1,738,984,000,000
Intangible	$1,535,857,000,000
Total Money (M0)	$3,274,841,000,000

M0 plus all bank account money is referred to as "M3". This is no longer published by the Fed, but is estimated[5] at $17,682,335,000,000. The total amount of credit extended in U.S. Dollars can be estimated from the sum of Dollar-denominated money accounts[6], bonds[7], public equities[8] and private equities[9].

Reference

[1] https://en.wikipedia.org/wiki/Money_supply#United_States

[2] https://en.wikipedia.org/wiki/Money_supply#Money_creation_by_commercial_banks

[3] Chapter: State Banking Principle

[4] https://www.federalreserve.gov/releases/h3/current/default.htm

[5] https://fred.stlouisfed.org/series/MABMM301USM189S

[6] https://en.wikipedia.org/wiki/Bank_account

[7] https://www.forbes.com/sites/kevinmcpartland/2018/10/11/understanding-us-bond-market/

[8] https://data.worldbank.org/indicator/cm.mkt.lcap.cd

[9] https://www.quora.com/What-is-the-estimated-total-value-of-all-US-private-companies

Dollar Credit	Amount (2019)
Bank (M3-M0)	$14,407,494,000,000
Bond	$41,000,000,000,000
Public Equity	$32,891,169,631,125
Private Equity	$6,426,333,525,358

From the table:

- The total ratio of money to credit is ~3.46%, or credit expansion of 29.9 x money.

- Bank reserves[1] of $1,400,949,000,000 indicate a bank reserve ratio of ~11.11% against bank credit, or credit expansion of 9.0 x money. This is slightly above the required reserve[2] ratio, which is no more than 10%[3].

- Reserve of remaining money (i.e. excluding bank reserves) relative to bond and equity markets (i.e. the ratio of M0 minus bank reserves to the sum of bonds and equity) is ~2.08%, or credit expansion of 48.0 x money.

Eliminating credit expansion requires elimination of credit, and therefore production. All credit is subject to default. However the theory holds that bank credit is different in the presumption of being "risk free". This presumption arises from the fact of taxpayer insurance[4] of the credit. This is not a consequence of banking but of state intervention in banking. To the extent the presumption is attributed to free banking[5], the theory is

Reference

[1] https://www.federalreserve.gov/releases/h3/current/default.htm
[2] https://en.wikipedia.org/wiki/Reserve_requirement
[3] https://en.wikipedia.org/wiki/Reserve_requirement#United_States
[4] https://www.fdic.gov
[5] https://en.wikipedia.org/wiki/Free_banking

invalid. All classes of business are subject to failure, and in doing so free banking eliminates this misperception.

The distinction between a money market fund[1] (MMF) and a money market account[2] (MMA) is informative. Both are intended to maintain a one-to-one equivalence with money, yet both are discounted against money due to settlement[3] and risk costs (e.g. some people accept only money, rejecting the higher costs of credit card[4] and cheque[5] transactions). The distinction (apart from taxpayer insurance of the latter) is in the treatment of investment risk and of insufficient reserve.

In the case of a MMF, investment failure is reflected in unit pricing. While the fund attempts to maintain sufficient net asset value[6] (NAV) to allow exchange a unit of the fund for one of the money, a sufficient drop in NAV will be reflected in unit price. In the case of an MMA, such losses are absorbed by money reserves. If there is insufficient reserve, either because of an unexpected level of withdrawal, or because of investment losses, the MMA fails. Failure of an MMA manifests as a bank run[7], where some people are repaid and others not. Insufficient NAV of a MMF manifests as a uniform drop in unit price.

The advantage of the MMA is that its units are more fungible[8], though still discounted against money. The advantage of the MMF is that losses are evenly spread. It is not surprising therefore that MMAs are typically insured by the taxpayer, more tightly

Reference

[1] https://en.wikipedia.org/wiki/Money_market_fund
[2] https://en.wikipedia.org/wiki/Money_market_account
[3] https://en.wikipedia.org/wiki/Settlement
[4] https://en.wikipedia.org/wiki/Credit_card
[5] https://en.wikipedia.org/wiki/Cheque
[6] https://en.wikipedia.org/wiki/Net_asset_value
[7] https://en.wikipedia.org/wiki/Bank_run
[8] https://en.wikipedia.org/wiki/Fungibility

regulated by the state, and accounted for as bank credit. It is rare for a MMF to "break the buck"[1] but of course it can and does happen. Bank failures also happen but are hidden by taxpayer insurance.

Bank credit is not truly fungible. This can be seen in everyday use of credit cards and cheques. There is a material risk of failure to settle associated with each. While this risk is generally attributed to the account holder (e.g. in the case of an MMA), it is a non-distinction to the person accepting the credit. One might imagine therefore that the acceptance of credit cards and cheques against MMFs to be treated similarly. The credit would circulate as a money-equivalent while more evenly distributing risk across those who are benefiting from its investment return. Free banking has the option to adopt either model to whatever extent people desire, but in any case credit will expand against money, risk will exist, and money substitutes[2] will exist.

The decision to hoard vs. invest[3] is based strictly on each person's time preference[4] Time preference is not derivable from any condition. It is, as the name implies, a human preference. Human preferences change and therefore so does time preference. Time preference determines the economic interest rate which can also be considered the cost of capital. An increase in the cost of capital resulting from increasing time preference causes credit available to contract, and a decrease has the opposite effect. With infinite time preference all capital would be hoarded for consumption, ending all production.

It matters not whether a lender is referred to as a "bank", all investment implies the same behavior. If banks operated with a 100% hoard they would not be lenders. This does not imply any reduction in lending, as the rate of lending[5] is determined by time preference

Reference

[1] https://www.investopedia.com/articles/mutualfund/08/money-market-break-buck.asp
[2] https://wiki.mises.org/wiki/Money_substitutes
[3] Chapter: Savings Relation
[4] https://en.wikipedia.org/wiki/Time_preference
[5] Chapter: Unlendable Money Fallacy

alone. Bitcoin can be lent and does nothing to limit credit expansion. The theory is therefore invalid.

Eliminating credit expansion is equivalent to the condition of infinite time preference, an infinite interest rate, no capital available for production, and no products available for consumption. In states where credit is limited or prohibited by statute (usury[1] laws), investment moves to equity instruments, loan sharking[2], or an end to production.

Reference

[1] https://en.wikipedia.org/wiki/Usury
[2] https://en.wikipedia.org/wiki/Loan_shark

Depreciation Principle

Ownership of a product moves from producer to consumer (or producer), yet neither production nor consumption[1] occurs at that time. The producer hoards the product before the trade and the consumer hoards it after. The product exists and is eventually traded between people. The terms "producer" and "consumer" are names for the *objectives* (production and leisure) of the two primary economic actors. The producer *intends* to create (appreciate) capital, while the consumer intends to destroy (depreciate) it. A producer who only owns does not produce and a consumer who does not own does not consume. But the producer's hoard (inventory) depreciates the product just as does the consumer's.

The common use of the term "consumption" conflates interest and depreciation[2]. The fact of a product sale represents interest to the investor, not depreciation of the product. The depreciation of a product is *actual* consumption, and represents either the extraction of service to its owner[3] (utility) or waste[4]. Waste is depreciation on which the owner places no value. Only destruction reflects actual consumption just as only creation reflects actual production. Only *action* is economically meaningful, the name of a given role is not. The net proceeds of a sale from producer to consumer is interest, even if it is capitalized through reinvestment.

Wealth, defined as capital accumulated, is the sum of products. All products are always hoarded and depreciating. Production creates products, where interest is both the cost of, and return on, doing so. The price of a product is the sum of its interest return on investment and the cost of all products consumed in its production. Any product

Reference

[1] Chapter: Production and Consumption

[2] https://en.wikipedia.org/wiki/Depreciation_(economics)

[3] https://mises.org/library/man-economy-and-state-power-and-market/html/p/974

[4] https://en.wikipedia.org/wiki/Waste

incorporated into a new product component is fully depreciated as an independent product and appreciated in the new product. Given that the sum of production costs equates to investment principal[1], the net increase in products is simply interest.

The rate of growth in wealth is the difference between the interest rate and the depreciation rate.

```
growth-rate = interest-rate - depreciation-rate
```

The following examples demonstrate the effect of depreciation on growth:

```
growth-rate = interest-rate - depreciation-rate
5% = 10% - 5%
-10% = 10% - 20%
```

The depreciation rate is always positive, as all property depreciates.

```
depreciation-rate > 0
interest-rate - growth-rate = depreciation-rate
interest-rate - growth-rate > 0
interest-rate > growth-rate
```

All property exhibits depreciation, which implies economic interest is always greater than economic growth.

The economic interest rate can be observed over time as the return on capital invested.[2]

Investors expect returns of 10.2% with millennials hoping for more.

Shroders: Global Investor Study

Reference

[1] https://en.wikipedia.org/wiki/Bond_(finance)#Principal

[2] https://www.schroders.com/en/insights/global-investor-study/investors-expect-returns-of-10.2-with-millennials-hoping-for-more

The depreciation rate can be derived from observed interest and capital growth rates.[1]

Global growth in 2019 has been downgraded to 2.6 percent, [...] reflecting weaker-than expected international trade and investment at the start of the year. Growth is projected to gradually rise to 2.8 percent by 2021.

World Bank: Global Economic Prospects

In this case an interest rate of 10.2% is offset by 7.6% depreciation to obtain 2.6% growth.

```
depreciation-rate = interest-rate - growth-rate depreciation-rate
10.2% - 2.6% = 7.6%
```

This is consistent with estimates of capital depreciation. While buildings and machinery have low rates of depreciation, vehicles, office equipment and food stocks (for example) have much higher.[2]

For the period 1960-2000, the three estimates for machinery and equipment are 5.61%, 5.42%, and 5.68%. For buildings, the estimates 3.36%, 3.43%, and 3.43%.

OECD: Estimating Depreciation Rates

Reference

[1] https://www.worldbank.org/en/publication/global-economic-prospects

[2] https://www.oecd.org/sdd/productivity-stats/35409605.pdf

To the extent money[1] exhibits use value[2], it depreciates as any good[3]. Fiat money, such as Bitcoin or the U.S. Dollar, is presumed to have no use value. A pure money exhibits no growth due to the opportunity cost[4] of interest foregone. In other words, interest is the capture of time value and money depreciation includes the failure to capture that value.

```
pure-money-growth-rate = interest-rate - interest-rate
9% - 9% = 0%
```

All actual money value also depreciates due to demurrage[5].

```
commodity-money-growth-rate = pure-money-growth-rate - demurrage-rate
0% - 1% = -1%
```

Growth rates of inflationary[6] and deflationary money are shown in Unlendable Money Fallacy[7].

Reference

[1] Chapter: Money Taxonomy

[2] https://en.wikipedia.org/wiki/Use_value

[3] https://en.wikipedia.org/wiki/Goods

[4] https://en.wikipedia.org/wiki/Opportunity_cost

[5] https://en.wikipedia.org/wiki/Demurrage_(currency)

[6] https://en.wikipedia.org/wiki/Monetary_inflation

[7] Chapter: Unlendable Money Fallacy

Expression Principle

Human actions should not be conflated with goods. The failure to distinguish between the two, at the most fundamental level, leads to errors of significant consequence[1]. Actions are fundamentally human preferences given expression through goods, which are the objects of that expression. Without expression, a preference is merely a thought and a good provides no service. Catallactics[2] concerns itself with expressed preferences, specifically production[3], trade, and consumption[4].

The human spirit is the actor (person). It has preferences that it expresses by motivating the body over which it has control (owns). This body is its property, a good. When its body is fully depreciated (dead), the spirit ceases to be an actor. It is not necessary to contemplate disembodied spirits, as no action is implied.

Catallactics is not concerned with legal, theological, or ethical concepts of humanity. The Turing Test[5] is sufficient criteria for the definition of humanity. The catallactic distinction is in the formation of preferences, independent of any other actor. A person in this sense is a decision-maker, as distinct from a rule-follower. A machine is a good that expresses the preferences of a person. A person expresses its preferences by motivating its machine.

A spirit cannot be property, and a body is the property of its spirit. Only the spirit controls the body, where control defines ownership. Where the spirit is compelled to act through

Reference

[1] https://en.m.wikipedia.org/wiki/Labor_theory_of_value
[2] https://en.m.wikipedia.org/wiki/Catallactics
[3] Chapter: Production and Consumption
[4] Chapter: Depreciation Principle
[5] https://en.m.wikipedia.org/wiki/Turing_test

the aggression[1] of another actor, the preference is not independent. The preference expressed (action) is that of the aggressor.

Catallactics considers only the consequences of independent actors. When a person suffers theft, the thief's preference is expressed, not his own. When a person pays a tax, he is presumed to be expressing the preference of another person, as tax is involuntary by nature. Slavery implies expression of the slaver's preferences, not those of the slave. The substitution of one's preference for that of another is involuntary trade (theft).

It is sometimes argued that time is valuable because life is temporary. This is not the basis of time preference[2]. The impermanence of a person is of no consequence to catallactics. A person may live forever yet is still presumed to exhibit a preference for goods sooner than later. Infinite life does not imply no desire to consume.

Action is the expression of human preference through goods. Processes directed by humans are action, processes directed by machines are goods. In other words, production/labor[3], trade/theft, and leisure/waste are actions, while websites, assembly lines, and cars are goods.

Reference

[1] https://en.m.wikipedia.org/wiki/Non-aggression_principle
[2] Chapter: Time Preference Fallacy
[3] Chapter: Labor and Leisure

Full Reserve Fallacy

There is a theory that fractional reserve[1] banking is a fraud, allowing banks to create money[2] "out of thin air"[3]. The theory implies that honest banking must be full reserve[4].

This theory hinges on the definition of the word "bank". Rothbard[5] makes the above argument in *Man, Economy, and State*[6], but explicitly limits his definition of a bank[7] to that of a "warehouse" for money:

> When a man deposits goods at a warehouse, he is given a receipt and pays the owner of the warehouse a certain sum for the service of storage. He still retains ownership of the property; the owner of the warehouse is simply guarding it for him. When the warehouse receipt is presented, the owner is obligated to restore the good deposited. A warehouse specializing in money is known as a "bank."
>
> *Murray Rothbard: Man, Economy, and State*

Banks do offer this warehousing service, in the name of safe deposit[8]. But banks are not so narrowly defined. They also generally offer interest-bearing accounts such as saving deposit[9] and term deposit[10]. Rothbard uses the expectation of interest to differentiate warehousing money from lending it:

Reference

[1] https://en.wikipedia.org/wiki/Fractional-reserve_banking

[2] Chapter: Money Taxonomy

[3] Chapter: Thin Air Fallacy

[4] https://en.wikipedia.org/wiki/Full-reserve_banking

[5] https://en.wikipedia.org/wiki/Murray_Rothbard

[6] https://mises.org/library/man-economy-and-state-power-and-market/html

[7] https://mises.org/library/man-economy-and-state-power-and-market/html/pp/1086

[8] https://en.wikipedia.org/wiki/Safe_deposit_box

[9] https://en.wikipedia.org/wiki/Savings_account

[10] https://en.wikipedia.org/wiki/Time_deposit

> Someone else's property is taken by the warehouse and used for its own money-making purposes. It is not borrowed, since no interest is paid for the use of the money.

In other words, his call for full reserve does not apply to interest-bearing accounts. However he neglects to point out that interest earned on the money represented by deposits can legitimately offset otherwise necessary account fees.

Banks often offer demand deposit[1] (e.g. checking) accounts without interest. The fact of positive yield on the account is not the demarcation between warehousing and lending, even by his own definition. Where a bank account yields 5% at a fee rate of 6%, no distinction from 0% yield with a 1% fee rate exists. The distinction is the contractual agreement between the depositor and the bank.

> Since it is convenient to transfer paper in exchange rather than carry gold, money warehouses (or banks) that build up public confidence will find that few people redeem their certificates.

Money certificates representing warehoused money are representative money[2], a form of money substitute[3]. In the United States, state banks[4] and others formerly issued such certificates. These were eventually replaced by central bank[5] issued gold certificates[6] and silver certificates[7].

Reference

[1] https://en.wikipedia.org/wiki/Transaction_account

[2] https://en.wikipedia.org/wiki/Representative_money

[3] https://wiki.mises.org/wiki/Money_substitutes

[4] https://en.wikipedia.org/wiki/State_bank

[5] https://en.wikipedia.org/wiki/Central_bank

[6] https://en.wikipedia.org/wiki/Gold_certificate

[7] https://en.wikipedia.org/wiki/Silver_certificate

The banks will be particularly subject to the temptation to commit fraud and issue pseudo money certificates to circulate side by side with genuine money certificates as acceptable money-substitutes. The fact that money is a homogeneous good means that people do not care whether the money they redeem is the original money they deposited. This makes bank frauds easier to accomplish.

To the extent that central bank certificates ever represented all of the warehoused money (e.g. gold and silver), they eventually followed the course described by Rothbard.

As the sum of certificates became too large to support redeemability, they were abrogated and people were compelled[1] to convert them to fiat. These large scale frauds occurred in the lifetimes of both Rothbard and his precursor von Mises[2], and were perpetrated by state and central banks under the protection of statute (i.e. the state).

The theory does not limit its condemnation of banking to warehousing (safe deposit) fraud, it extends to honest lending of deposits by banks generally, including demand deposit, saving deposit and often term deposit. As such the theory is invalid. Furthermore it implies a condemnation of lending and investing generally. And as Rothbard himself points out[3], lending is indistinct from investing:

Whether saved capital is channeled into investments via stocks or via loans is unimportant. The only difference is in the legal technicalities. Indeed, even the legal difference between the creditor and the owner is a negligible one.

Reference

[1] https://en.wikipedia.org/wiki/Gold_Reserve_Act

[2] https://en.wikipedia.org/wiki/Ludwig_von_Mises

[3] https://mises.org/library/man-economy-and-state-power-and-market/html/p/996

All lending originates from a person's accumulated capital, whether deposited in bank or otherwise. There is no source for lending other than savings deposited. There is a related theory[1] that people are too stupid to understand contractual terms of deposit.

> Huerta de Soto considers the possibility "that a certain group of bank customers (or for the sake of argument, all of them) enter into a deposit contract aware and fully accepting that banks will invest (or loan, etc.) a large portion of the money they deposit". In this case, argues Huerta de Soto, "the supposed authorization from the depositors lacks legal validity" because few lay-persons understand the instability inherent in fractional-reserve banking: they believe their deposit is guaranteed, which Huerta de Soto considers a (near universal) misconception.
>
> *Wikipedia: Jesús Huerta de Soto*

Yet those who make this argument believe themselves able to understand it. As such the theory is invalid. Given the moral distinction of nonaggression[2], it is the right of every individual to contract with another voluntarily. Taking this right away would be the crime. References to the "unbanked" generally assume that vast numbers of people do not have "access" to banking services. This is generally not the case; banking is widely available all over the world. These are the people who understand the risks[3] and chose not to take them.

A related theory is that money substitutes trade at the same value as the money, representing a fraud. To the extent that money substitutes (e.g. deposit accounts) are insured by the taxpayer[4], the discount against the money they substitute is lower. However, even given full insurance, it is an error to assume these trade at par with the money. Money substitutes manifest as deposit accounts and are generally transacted

Reference

[1] https://en.wikipedia.org/wiki/Jes%C3%BAs_Huerta_de_Soto#Austrian_business_cycle_and_full _reserve_banking

[2] https://en.wikipedia.org/wiki/Non-aggression_principle

[3] https://www.reuters.com/article/zimbabwe-crisis-cbank/zimbabwe-c-bank-says-raided-private -bank-accounts-idUSLK23553320090420

[4] https://www.fdic.gov/

electronically. Settling[1] money accounts incurs time, money and risk costs. Credit card and cheque fraud is rampant[2], and this cost is surfaced in all transaction and account fees. Settling can take days[3] if not months[4]. Merchants necessarily discount money substitutes[5] against money. Even electronic transfer directly between banks incurs a material settlement cost[6]:

> Banks are charged a gross transfer fee of $0.82 for every transaction, however there is a three-tiered discount schedule, which results in actual transaction fees costing between $0.034 and $0.82 per transaction depending on transaction volume.
>
> *Wikipedia: Fedwire*

This is why many business are "cash only", others do not accept cheques, others charge a premium to offset the discount, and why there are ATM fees[7], etc. As such the observation that money substitutes are not discounted is refuted by a mountain of evidence to the contrary. More importantly, this discount is provably necessary, invalidating the theory.

A related theory is that bank lending creates price inflation[8] as a consequence of credit expansion[9]. Given that lending and money have necessarily evolved together, there is never a time where credit expansion itself changes the level of money substitutes. This requires either an expansion of the money supply[10], or a reduction in time preference[11],

Reference

[1] https://en.wikipedia.org/wiki/Settlement_(finance)

[2] https://en.wikipedia.org/wiki/Credit_card_fraud

[3] https://en.wikipedia.org/wiki/Cheque_clearing

[4] https://en.wikipedia.org/wiki/Chargeback

[5] https://en.wikipedia.org/wiki/Merchant_account#Discount_rates

[6] https://en.wikipedia.org/wiki/Fedwire

[7] https://en.wikipedia.org/wiki/ATM_usage_fees

[8] https://en.wikipedia.org/wiki/Inflation

[9] Chapter: Credit Expansion Fallacy

[10] https://en.wikipedia.org/wiki/Gold_mining

[11] Chapter: Time Preference Fallacy

reflected as the economic rate of interest. Credit expansion is strictly a function of these two factors, not lending itself. As such the theory is invalid.

A related theory is that banks may legitimately lend only "their own" money. All capital lent is someone's savings. If anyone can run a bank (i.e. borrow against their own savings and lend it to others) then this is a distinction without a difference. Aggregating savings with other people (i.e. through bank deposits) does not create any meaningful distinction. As such the theory is invalid.

A related theory is that banks may legitimately lend only against time deposits. There is no economic distinction between a time deposit and a demand deposit, as both imply fractional reserve. The nature of deposit, even safe deposit, implies that time and other constraints (e.g. identification) are required for withdrawal. Even taxpayer-insured checking and savings accounts are effectively time deposits[1]:

> For all savings accounts and all personal interest-bearing checking accounts, we reserve the right to require seven days' prior written notice of withdrawal.
>
> *Chase Bank: Deposit Agreement*

Default risk and credit expansion remain despite maturity matching. As such the theory is invalid. The only true demand deposit is no deposit at all (money), and of course people have this option and that of time deposit to the extent they prefer it.

A related theory is that banks may legitimately lend only against fully-insured deposits. However the only true risk free return[2] is no return. This is why only taxpayers insure loans (i.e. through compulsion). Full insurance is economically equivalent to no lending whatsoever, making the theory a contradiction, and therefore invalid.

Reference

[1] https://www.chase.com/content/dam/chasecom/en/checking/documents/deposit_account_ag reement.pdf

[2] Chapter: Risk Free Return Fallacy

A related theory is that even free banking[1] has an inherent ability to create money "out of thin air"[2]. Yet if this is true then anyone can do so, since free banking confers no special powers on people who refer to themselves as banks. If money can be created at no cost, it cannot be property. As such the theory is invalid. Even state fiat incurs a production cost[3], a cost to maintain its monopoly on production[4], and a political cost[5] of monetary inflation[6]. Free banking, such as with Gold or Bitcoin, enjoys no seigniorage[7] privilege, due to the nature of competition.

Finally, it is often the case that people advocating for full reserve lending are the same people advocating for lower time preferences. This is a direct contradiction, as the former implies infinite time preference.

Reference

[1] https://en.wikipedia.org/wiki/Free_banking

[2] Chapter: Thin Air Fallacy

[3] https://www.federalreserve.gov/faqs/currency_12771.htm

[4] https://en.wikipedia.org/wiki/Counterfeit

[5] https://en.wikipedia.org/wiki/Crisis_in_Venezuela

[6] https://en.wikipedia.org/wiki/Monetary_inflation

[7] https://en.wikipedia.org/wiki/Seigniorage

Inflation Principle

A money[1] is presumed[2] to change in purchasing power[3] in proportion to the demand for goods that it represents. In other words, with twice the amount of money each unit of the money will trade for half its previous amount of goods, as the increase in goods implies lower demand for them. This is a proportional relationship[4] between monetary inflation[5] and price inflation[6] (or deflation). This money relation[7] is an expression of the law of supply and demand[8].

- Rising supply market money, such as Gold and *early* Bitcoin, consumes the same value in goods as it creates in new units – including the opportunity cost[9] of the capital invested in doing so. As such it produces no change in proportionality and therefore no price inflation.

- Monopoly money is not subject to competitive production, allowing its producer to obtain a monopoly[10] premium in the pricing of new units. As such it increases the proportion of money to goods, resulting in price inflation.

- Fixed supply market money, such as late Bitcoin, creates no units. As such the proportion of money to goods decreases with economic growth, resulting in price deflation[11].

Reference

[1] Chapter: Money Taxonomy

[2] https://mises.org/library/man-economy-and-state-power-and-market/html/p/1107

[3] https://en.wikipedia.org/wiki/Purchasing_power

[4] https://en.wikipedia.org/wiki/Proportionality_(mathematics)

[5] https://en.wikipedia.org/wiki/Monetary_inflation

[6] https://en.wikipedia.org/wiki/Inflation

[7] https://mises.org/library/human-action-0/html/pp/778

[8] https://en.wikipedia.org/wiki/Supply_and_demand

[9] https://en.wikipedia.org/wiki/Opportunity_cost

[10] https://mises.org/library/man-economy-and-state-power-and-market/html/pp/1054

[11] https://en.wikipedia.org/wiki/Deflation

Proportionality refers to the goods "represented" by a money. If there was only one money, this would be a straightforward relation to all goods. However the relation must be addressed in the case of multiple monies. The goods represented by a money are those that it can be traded for. In other words, the relation implies demand for goods in the money.

Yet demand does not remain constant in the case of a decision to mine. New demand for goods is created by the fact of mining. The miner must consume "representation" goods in producing the money. The new money is entirely offset by the demand increase represented by the consumed goods and the opportunity cost (i.e. fewer new goods) of employing them in mining. Therefore proportionality is preserved in the case of multiple monies as well. **Economic growth is not price-inflationary in a free market.**

In expanding upon the Copernican[1] quantity theory of money[2], Richard Cantillon[3] formulated a theory now known as the Cantillon Effect[4]. The theory is valid when applied to monopoly monies, but has no relevance to market money – a fact that seems to have escaped economists since Cantillon. The basis of the distortions explained by Cantillon is seigniorage[5], not money production. Market production of money, just as market production of all things, is not only neutral in real effects[6] but also price neutral.

Reference

[1] https://en.wikipedia.org/wiki/Nicolaus_Copernicus
[2] https://en.wikipedia.org/wiki/Quantity_theory_of_money
[3] https://en.wikipedia.org/wiki/Richard_Cantillon
[4] https://en.wikipedia.org/wiki/Richard_Cantillon#Monetary_theory
[5] https://en.wikipedia.org/wiki/Seigniorage
[6] https://en.wikipedia.org/wiki/Neutrality_of_money

In *Human Action*[1], Ludwig von Mises[2], as his predecessors, attempts to demonstrate[3] the validity of the Cantillon Effect to *any* money.

> Changes in the supply of money must necessarily alter the disposition of vendible goods as owned by various individuals and firms. The quantity of money available in the whole market system cannot increase or decrease otherwise than by first increasing or decreasing the cash holdings of certain individual members.
>
> *Ludwig von Mises: Human Action*

This statement asserts that new money first effects existing money holdings. Yet this is not the case with market money. Its creation coincidentally *reduces goods holdings* as it *increases money holdings*. The increased demand for money is concurrently and proportionately offset by its increased supply. This reduction of goods cannot be ignored in evaluation of the money relation. The statement conflates market money with monopoly money, as the latter does not consume its value in goods through production. To the extent the goods are consumed in essentially the same location as money is produced, and at the same time, not even an uneven distribution of the money relation is implied. This error persists despite explicit recognition that mining consumes in goods the value that it produces in new money.

> The fact that the owners of gold mines rely upon steady yearly proceeds from their gold production does not cancel the newly mined gold's impression upon prices. The owners of the mines take from the market, in exchange for the gold produced, the goods and services required for their mining [...]. If they had not produced this amount of gold, prices would not have been affected by it.

Taken literally the last sentence is a tautology[4] (no creation implies no price effect from the creation). From the context it is clear Mises intends that, had the gold not been

Reference

[1] https://mises.org/library/human-action-0/html
[2] https://en.wikipedia.org/wiki/Ludwig_von_Mises
[3] https://mises.org/library/human-action-0/html/pp/778
[4] https://en.wikipedia.org/wiki/Tautology_(logic)

produced, prices would be unchanged. Yet without a change to the money supply, had the goods been consumed in other production[1], the implied economic growth would *decrease* prices; and if the goods had been consumed in leisure[2], the implied economic contraction would *increase* prices. In other words, the above conclusion is perfectly reversed. The money relation is *preserved* because of money production and would change due to lack thereof. This error then infects dependent theories.

> As against this reasoning one must first of all observe that within a progressing economy in which population figures are increasing and the division of labor and its corollary, industrial specialization, are perfected, there prevails a tendency toward an increase in the demand for money. Additional people appear on the scene and want to establish cash holdings. The extent of economic self-sufficiency, i.e., of production for the household's own needs, shrinks and people become more dependent upon the market; this will, by and large, [p. 415] impel them to increase their holding of cash.

In other words, economic growth alone changes the money relation – a direct contradiction of the preceding statement.

> Thus the price-raising tendency emanating from what is called the "normal" gold production encounters a price-cutting tendency emanating from the increased demand for cash holding. However, these two opposite tendencies do not neutralize each other. Both processes take their own course, both result in a disarrangement of existing social conditions, making some people richer, some people poorer. Both affect the prices of various goods at different dates and to a different degree. It is true that the rise in the prices of some commodities caused by one of these processes can finally be compensated by the fall caused by the other process. It may happen that at the end some or many prices come back to their previous height. But this final result is not the outcome of an absence of movements provoked by changes in the money relation. It is rather the outcome of the joint effect of the coincidence of two processes independent of each other.

This is a refutation of the idea of money creation as a "stimulus"[3] to growth, which is correct. Yet it incorrectly assumes money demand and money creation are independent

Reference

[1] Chapter: Production and Consumption

[2] Chapter: Labor and Leisure

[3] https://en.wikipedia.org/wiki/Stimulus_(economics)

processes. They are explicitly dependent as expressed in the money relation and the law of supply and demand which it echoes. The effect of unrelated interactions is perfectly reversed in this argument, as it can only mask the money relation. Stimulus is a reversal of cause and effect, properly refuted, yet it is an error to both accept the money relation and reject it.

The underlying inflation error, like that of the regression theorem[1], may arise from an understandable desire to explain the adverse effects[2] of monopoly money. Yet in the purely rational system of catallactics[3], any error in deduction produces inconsistency, which is evident in this case. Market money is subject to monetary inflation, yet produces no price inflation. Monopoly money is similarly subject to monetary inflation, but produces price inflation – solely due to the monopoly on production. Mises overgeneralizes that *all* monetary inflation is price inflationary.

> Prices also rise in the same way if [...] the demand for money falls because of a general tendency toward a diminution of cash holdings. The money expended additionally by such a "dishoarding" brings about a tendency toward higher prices in the same way as that flowing from the gold mines [...]. Conversely, prices drop when the supply of money falls [when] the demand for money increases (e.g., through a tendency toward "hoarding," the keeping of greater cash balances).

All money is always owned by someone. Under the above assumption of no money creation, a greater "cash balance" for one person implies a lesser for another. Increased money hoarding implies only a decreased present demand for goods relative to anticipated future demand. Decreased hoarding implies only increased present demand for goods. It is not as if money has been sewn back into the earth. There is no cost of "dishoarding" (trading the money), so doing so is unlike money "flowing from the gold mines".

Reference

[1] Chapter: Regression Fallacy

[2] https://en.wikipedia.org/wiki/Seigniorage

[3] https://en.wikipedia.org/wiki/Catallactics

A generally increased level of hoarding gives the *impression* of greater wealth, but this is illusory. In order to be of value to people money must be traded for goods, at which point the illusion evaporates. Unlike with mining, the effect of dishoarding is uneven. The first to do so obtains the highest exchange value and the last the lowest. The speculative[1] strategy of "pump and dump"[2] is based on exploiting this unevenness. Wealth is transferred, not created.

Furthermore, increased hoarding implies higher time preference[3], which is the ratio of hoarded capital to lent capital (capital ratio[4]), reflected as the interest rate. This is increased time cost, not increased capital value. The same amount of goods exist (wealth) at the point where hoarding increases. Yet this increase proportionally reduces production, due to increased cost of capital. This creates a *permanent* and compounding reduction in wealth, as the time lost in production is never recovered even with subsequent dishoarding. If all money was hoarded for a decade (assuming no reversion to barter), people may dishoard only to find their money has lost significant value due to the dramatic reduction in the amount of goods.

Independent of economic growth (or contraction), a change in demand for a market money implies a proportional change in demand for, or supply of, goods traded for the money, as opposed to another money or barter. The supply of goods is the level to which the money is accepted in trade for them. A money exhibits monetary value only in its ability be directly or indirectly exchanged for things of use value[5], as directly implied by the money relation itself. The value of a money derives from people willing to accept it

Reference

[1] Chapter: Speculative Consumption

[2] https://en.wikipedia.org/wiki/Pump_and_dump

[3] Chapter: Time Preference Fallacy

[4] Chapter: Savings Relation

[5] https://en.wikipedia.org/wiki/Use_value

in trade (i.e. the economy). Given the fungibility[1] of money, selling the money[2] to another person implies no change to this acceptance.

To the extent it pertains to commodity money, this principle assumes that the amount of goods required to produce the money remains constant. The price of goods in the money is thereby held constant by the money relation. However, where the value of goods required to produce a commodity money increases or decreases, decrease or increase of prices in the money is implied respectively. Therefore, independent of demand, the money relation is controlled by the rate of change in necessary production factors. Such changes are presumed to be unpredictable, as otherwise they are already incorporated into price. As such this constitutes speculative error.

Reference

[1] https://en.m.wikipedia.org/wiki/Fungibility
[2] Chapter: Dumping Fallacy

Labor and Leisure

Labor and leisure are complementary human actions[1] that pertain to production and consumption[2] of economic goods[3]. Labor is the process of consumption to produce an economic good (production). Leisure is the process of consumption that does not produce an economic good. Consumption without utility is the process of waste[4]. According to Murray Rothbard[5], in his *Man, Economy and State*[6]:

> labor always involves the forgoing of leisure, a desirable good
>
> *Murray Rothbard: Man Economy and State*

This subtle error implies that both labor and leisure are economic goods. Yet only actions create or consume goods[7]. Labor (production of economic goods) and leisure (production of non-economic goods) are human actions that create and consume goods over time. In the most basic sense, production implies the consumption of the actor's body, while consumption implies its production.

Reference

[1] https://en.wikipedia.org/wiki/Action_axiom

[2] Chapter: Production and Consumption

[3] https://en.m.wikipedia.org/wiki/Goods_and_services

[4] https://en.wikipedia.org/wiki/Waste

[5] https://en.wikipedia.org/wiki/Murray_Rothbard

[6] https://mises.org/library/man-economy-and-state-power-and-market/html/p/926

[7] Chapter: Expression Principle

In each hour he will expend his effort toward producing that good whose marginal product is highest on his value scale. If he must give up an hour of labor, he will give up a unit of that good whose marginal utility is lowest on his value scale. At each point he will balance the utility of the product on his value scale against the disutility of further work. We know that a man's marginal utility of goods provided by effort will decline as his expenditure of effort increases. On the other hand, with each new expenditure of effort, the marginal disutility of the effort continues to increase. Therefore, a man will expend his labor as long as the marginal utility of the return exceeds the marginal disutility of the labor effort. A man will stop work when the marginal disutility of labor is greater than the marginal utility of the increased goods provided by the effort.

Then, as his consumption of leisure increases, the marginal utility of leisure will decline, while the marginal utility of the goods forgone increases, until finally the utility of the marginal products forgone becomes greater than the marginal utility of leisure, and the actor will resume labor again.

This analysis of the laws of labor effort has been deduced from the implications of the action axiom and the assumption of leisure as a consumers' good.

It is neither correct nor necessary to assume leisure is a good, and by doing so imply that labor is an anti-good. It is similarly not necessary to construct the artifice of negative utility ("disutility"). Value is simply a preference for higher utility over lower utility. Both labor and leisure produce goods of (positive) utility.

It is time preference[1] that implies leisure utility is greater than labor utility. By properly accounting for a person's body as property, "leisure preference" follows directly from time preference. As the above quote implies, this is the result of a trade of time without one's body (labor time) for the amount of interest that offsets the value one attributes to time with his body (leisure time).

Time, space and goods are the factors of all production, while labor is the process of production. **Labor/leisure and production are distinct names for the same human action.** The act of producing is labor or leisure; the act of laboring or leisuring is

Reference

[1] Chapter: Time Preference Fallacy

production. The Pure Bank[1] provides the model of all production. This cycle is clearly evident in the case of self-employment, which is just the example of production. In the case of a wage-earner there are two producers, the employee and the employer.

A pure wage-earning employee obtains borrowed capital and thereby trades for food, education, and equipment, as required for a job. A fraction of his capital is hoarded and the rest is lent to the employer. The employer pays the employee interest (wages) for the term of this loan. The employee recovers his depreciated principal and wage at the end of the job.

The wage rate offsets both time preference for the lent amount (nominal interest rate) and principal depreciation during the term of the loan. The amount of principal and interest, less depreciation of the fraction reserved, is returned to the employee's creditor. In the case where his capital investment is borrowed from his own hoard, the employee is his own creditor. The return is then hoarded or reinvested in future labor (or otherwise).

A real employer and employee each obtain a market rate of interest. The employee's interest rate is his wage rate less his production expense. The employer's interest rate is the price obtained for the work product over the time of its production less his production expense. The employer's production expense is the consumption of his borrowed capital, reserved[2] over that time, just as for the employee. The amount by which interest exceeds depreciation is the increase in wealth[3] to both parties.

The interest rate obtained by both classes of production is the same. The difference in amounts returned is strictly a function of the amount of capital invested, either in individual production (employee) or in managing collective production (employer). A

Reference

[1] Chapter: Pure Bank
[2] Chapter: Reservation Principle
[3] Chapter: Depreciation Principle

person's maximum leisure valuation can be inferred from the wage rate he accepts, by discounting[1] the implied principal by the market interest rate.

```
wage-rate = leisure-rate * (1 + interest-rate + body-depreciation-rate)
```

The employee trades leisure time for labor time to the extent that he values the amount of interest more than the value he attributes to leisure time. Leisure preference is a restatement of time preference, where one's own body is the economic good being lent to production in exchange for interest.

Money wealth is generally lower at an early age, implying a higher money time preference. Over time wealth accumulates and time preference decreases. But the opposite is true with leisure preference. Money and one's body are not the same property, and are not generally exchangeable. At an early age, one has the lowest leisure preference. As one's body depreciates with age, the amount of it declines despite money wealth, increasing leisure preference. This may eventually require a higher-than-market interest rate to offset the preference, resulting in retirement. Money time preference and leisure preference affect each other as they tend to move in opposite directions. To the extent that the objective of labor is to increase wealth, less wealth decreases leisure time preference and more increases it. This may also result in retirement.

Reference

[1] https://en.m.wikipedia.org/wiki/Present_value

Production and Consumption

Production and consumption are the complementary human actions[1] of producing and consuming economic goods[2]. The human roles of producer and consumer should not be conflated[3] with the acts of production and consumption. A role refers to intent not action. All producers consume and all consumers produce. Consumption that produces an economic good is production, otherwise it is the process of either leisure[4] or waste[5].

The Pure Bank[6] provides the model of all production. A pure producer has borrowed capital, consuming it in the creation of a product. The consumed fraction at any time has been lent to production. The unconsumed fraction at any time has been reserved[7] for liquidity. The new product is sold, obtaining interest on the consumed fraction, returned as dividend[8]. The amount of reserve is the same necessary productive expense as the Pure Bank's liquidity reserve. **The reserve is only repopulated by more borrowed capital, including dividend/earnings reinvestment.**

A real producer converts time and capital to interest, at the market price of the product produced, just as a real bank obtains interest at the market price. The bank is merely obtaining the interest of another producer by being its investor. This shows the fundamental equivalence of lending as debt and equity, independent of *statutory* distinctions (tax).

Reference

[1] https://en.wikipedia.org/wiki/Action_axiom
[2] https://en.m.wikipedia.org/wiki/Goods_and_services
[3] Chapter: Depreciation Principle
[4] Chapter: Labor and Leisure
[5] https://en.wikipedia.org/wiki/Waste
[6] Chapter: Pure Bank
[7] Chapter: Reserve Definition
[8] https://en.m.wikipedia.org/wiki/Dividend

A pure consumer hoards capital without any lent to production. All capital is borrowed and reserved. At 100% reserve there is no interest, no return, and eventually full depreciation. In this case the borrowed capital is considered a gift (charity[1]). A real consumer is additionally subject to tax and subsidy, which increases and decreases the rate of hoard depreciation respectively.

Reference

[1] https://en.wikipedia.org/wiki/Charity_(practice)

Pure Bank

The concept of a Pure Bank can be useful in demonstrating lending behavior generally.

A Pure Bank provides only the following services:

- borrows money (debt from creditors)
- lends money (credit from debtors)
- hoards money (reserve)

The material differences from a real bank are:

- no state intervention (free bank)
- no cost of operation (perfectly efficient)

The bank is owned by its creditors in proportion to their credit, as is the case with any company. There are existing major banks that are owned by their account holders, such as USAA[1] and Vanguard[2], so this is not a distinction from a real bank. Neither a Pure Bank nor a real bank has "own capital" to lend, as all capital is borrowed from investors in one form or another. The objective of creditors is to maximize their rate of return. The objective of debtors is to minimize their interest expense.

Creditor accounts are money substitutes[3]. This aspect distinguishes the bank from an investment fund. The money substitute may be either a demand deposit[4] or a money market[5]. The distinction is in the allocation of insufficient reserve (negative rate of

Reference

[1] https://www.usaa.com
[2] https://investor.vanguard.com
[3] https://wiki.mises.org/wiki/Money_substitutes
[4] https://en.wikipedia.org/wiki/Demand_deposit
[5] https://en.wikipedia.org/wiki/Money_market_fund

return), with the former being "first come, first served"[1] and the latter "breaking the buck"[2].

The lack of state intervention is the common concept of free banking[3], where there is no statutory control[4], state insurance[5], discount capital[6], or seigniorage[7]. The bank uses commodity money[8] unless otherwise specified, which simplifies calculations by eliminating[9] the need to offset price inflation[10] or price deflation[11].

Perfect efficiency differs from a real bank only in the rate of return, as nothing is consumed in operations. All earning is a consequence of time preference[12]. Uniform interest is assumed, as rate arbitrage[13] is an expense. Demurrage[14] is the expense of storing money. The expense ratio (inclusive of demurrage) is 1 for the Pure Bank.

Reference

[1] https://en.wikipedia.org/wiki/Bank_run
[2] https://en.wikipedia.org/wiki/Money_market_fund#Breaking_the_buck
[3] https://en.wikipedia.org/wiki/Free_banking
[4] https://en.wikipedia.org/wiki/Federal_Reserve
[5] https://www.fdic.gov
[6] https://en.wikipedia.org/wiki/Discount_window
[7] https://en.wikipedia.org/wiki/Seigniorage
[8] Chapter: Money Taxonomy
[9] Chapter: Inflation Principle
[10] https://en.wikipedia.org/wiki/Inflation
[11] https://en.wikipedia.org/wiki/Deflation
[12] Chapter: Time Preference Fallacy
[13] https://en.m.wikipedia.org/wiki/Arbitrage
[14] https://en.wikipedia.org/wiki/Demurrage_(currency)

Reserved capital is the money in which credit and debt are settled[1] (zero maturity[2]). Depreciation[3] is the opportunity cost[4] of it not being lent, also known as "cash drag". Interest relations assume a single compounding period[5] with the rate of interest over that period. This presentation simplification is inconsequential to implied relations.

Given the preceding definition of a Pure Bank, the following relations are absolute.

```
reserved = borrowed - lent
demurrage = demurrage-rate * reserved
depreciation = interest-rate * reserved
interest = interest-rate * lent
return = expense-ratio * interest
```

For the Pure Bank, the reserve ratio[6] fully determines capital ratio[7], debt ratio[8], and savings ratio.

Reserve Ratio

```
reserve-ratio = reserved / borrowed
reserve-ratio = (borrowed - lent) / borrowed
```


Reference

[1] https://en.wikipedia.org/wiki/Settlement_(finance)

[2] https://en.wikipedia.org/wiki/Maturity_(finance)

[3] Chapter: Depreciation Principle

[4] https://en.wikipedia.org/wiki/Opportunity_cost

[5] https://en.wikipedia.org/wiki/Compound_interest

[6] https://en.wikipedia.org/wiki/Reserve_requirement

[7] https://en.wikipedia.org/wiki/Capital_requirement

[8] https://en.wikipedia.org/wiki/Debt_ratio

Capital Ratio

```
capital-ratio = reserved / lent
capital-ratio = (borrowed - lent) / lent
```

Debt Ratio

```
debt-ratio = borrowed / reserved
debt-ratio = borrowed / (borrowed - lent)
```

Savings Ratio

```
savings-ratio = lent / reserved
savings-ratio = lent / (borrowed - lent)
```

Balance Sheet

The Pure Bank has no liabilities, only shareholder equity.

bank assets	shareholder equity
lent + reserved	borrowed

Rate of Return

Creditor rate of return is additionally a function of the interest rate. The creditor's rate of return is less than the debtor's interest rate due to cash drag, the necessary expense of demand withdrawal. To reduce this expense, time constraints are typically included in real bank contracts[1]. For example, by law any withdrawal from an interest-bearing U.S. bank account can be delayed for seven days. The creditor can only eliminate cash drag[2] by investing directly (i.e. without settlement assurances).

```
return-rate = interest-rate * lent / borrowed
```

As shown in Savings Relation[3] individual capital ratios fully determine the market interest rate. When we consider every person operating as a pure bank, it becomes clear that the capital ratio determines the interest rate. A capital ratio of 0% for all people implies that capital is free and has no return. At increasing capital ratios, the interest rate increases accordingly. At full hoarding the cost of capital is "infinite" – none can be obtained for production.

The presumption of the money relation[4] is that price is proportional to the ratio of demand to supply. But as shown in Savings Relation, supply and demand for capital exist in a zero-sum relation. An increase in hoarding implies a corresponding decrease in lending and the reverse implies an increase. As such neither the capital ratio nor the interest rate is linear in relation to change in the amount hoarded (or lent). This has led some to search for a "golden ratio"[5]. Yet given the subjectivity of value, this is ultimately an exercise in futility.

Yet capital ratios fully determine the interest rate. As all people individually attempt to obtain a golden ratio based on their own preferences, the market rate of interest results. Substituting the capital ratio for the interest rate demonstrates the effect of reservation

Reference

[1] https://www.chase.com/content/dam/chasecom/en/checking/documents/deposit_account_ag reement.pdf

[2] https://www.investopedia.com/terms/p/performance_drag.asp

[3] Chapter: Savings Relation

[4] Chapter: Inflation Principle

[5] https://en.wikipedia.org/wiki/Golden_Rule_savings_rate

on the Pure Bank, under the additional assumption that everyone operates as a Pure Bank and with the same capital ratio. The capital ratio includes present goods depreciation, which for money is demurrage. The Pure Bank demurrage ratio is 1, so this drops out.

```
return-rate = (reserved * demurrage-ratio / lent) * (lent / borrowed)
return-rate = (reserved / borrowed) * demurrage-ratio
return-rate = reserved / borrowed
```

The rate of return on Pure Bank investment becomes the reserve ratio. This does not imply that an individual Pure Bank can set its own return by setting its capital ratio. It merely reflects that the market capital ratio determines the return on capital. If *all lenders* doubled their present capital ratio their returns would necessarily double, as the cost for capital, and therefore its return, would double.

Real Banks

The independent capital ratios of all people, based on individual time preference, determine the market rate of interest. The above substitution for the bank's own capital ratio as the interest rate seems to imply that the bank is setting the interest rate. However this is inherent in the concept of time preference. A bank can set any level of interest it prefers. There is no assumption for real banks that the market will oblige, so market interest and therefore market returns are assumed.

```
market-return-rate = market-interest-rate * (lent / borrowed)
market-return-rate = market-capital-ratio * (lent / borrowed)
```

The Free Bank also differs from the Pure Bank by operational expense, which directly reduces rate of return.

```
free-bank-return-rate = market-return-rate * expense-ratio
```

The Real Bank only differs from the free bank by tax (inclusive of regulatory expense), which directly reduces rate of return.

```
real-return-rate = free-bank-return-rate * tax-expense-ratio
```

The Central Bank (state) only differs from the real bank by taxpayer subsidy (inclusive of discounted borrowing), which directly increases rate of return.

```
central-return-rate = real-bank-return-rate * subsidy-income-ratio
```

Where tax includes seigniorage of the bank money, the Fisher Equation[1] must be applied above to translate the interest rate from a nominal rate to a real rate. No other change is implied other than tax, which is accounted for by the Real Bank above. This tax is generally the source of subsidy, which is accounted for by the Central Bank above.

Every person, or company of people, is a Real Bank, and the state is a Central Bank. A Real Bank produces the service of liquid investment, an economic good[2]. The cost of production is the depreciation of its reserve. This is the model of all production.

Reference

[1] https://en.wikipedia.org/wiki/Fisher_equation

[2] https://en.wikipedia.org/wiki/Goods

Savings Relation

Time preference[1] is the catallactic[2] assumption of human preference for present goods over future goods. It is well established that time preference is reflected as the interest rate. According to Murray Rothbard[3], in his *Man, Economy and State*[4]:

> The level of the pure rate of interest is determined by the market for the exchange of present goods against future goods, a market which we shall see permeates many parts of the economic system. [...] Thus, if, on the time market, 100 ounces of gold exchange for the prospect of obtaining 105 ounces of gold one year from now, then the rate of interest is approximately 5 percent per annum. This is the time-discount rate of future to present money. [...] The pure rate of interest will then be the going rate of time discount, the ratio of the price of present goods to that of future goods.
>
> *Murray Rothbard: Man Economy and State*

However, it is individual capital ratio[5] that *determines* the interest rate. The interest ratio is that of future to present good price. It is the market price premium required to compensate an owner for time without his good – or the price of time. As with all prices, it is determined entirely by individual preferences, in its case time preference, expressed[6] as individual trades.

The time preference of an individual can be represented as the ratio of the price of his hoard to that of his lending. Together these amounts are his savings. In trading a fraction of his hoard for its future value, one expresses that its future amount is worth more to him than presently. Conversely, by not doing so one expresses the opposite valuation.

Reference

[1] Chapter: Time Preference Fallacy

[2] https://en.wikipedia.org/wiki/Catallactics

[3] https://en.wikipedia.org/wiki/Murray_Rothbard

[4] https://mises.org/library/man-economy-and-state-power-and-market/html/p/989

[5] https://en.wikipedia.org/wiki/Capital_requirement

[6] Chapter: Expression Principle

A hoard is the opportunity to invest (lend) and an investment is the opportunity to consume. One is traded for the other until no further increase in value is obtained from doing so. By investing, one values the future amount more than the present amount not invested. By not investing, one values the present amount not invested more than the future amount. If this were not the case there would be a lower or higher level of investment respectively. This valuation, manifested as a trade, is the expression of one's time preference.

> Perhaps more fallacies have been committed in discussions concerning the interest rate than in the treatment of any other aspect of economics. It took a long while for the crucial importance of time preference in the determination of the pure rate of interest to be realized in economics; it took even longer for economists to realize that time preference is the only determining factor. Reluctance to accept a monistic causal interpretation has plagued economics to this day.

The *individual* does not control the market interest rate. The individual controls his capital ratio given the market interest rate. The capital ratio is how individual time preference is *expressed*. The interest rate is how those preferences are *priced* by the market.

The following vertical bar chart provides an example of an individual's savings.

```
            Individual Capital Ratio (time preference)
             |
             |
    21 [     |
    20 [ H   |
    19 [ HH  |
   ---[----+--------------------- Market Interest (time price)
U  18 [ HHH|TTTTTTTTTTTTTTTTTT
N  17 [ HHH|PTTTTTTTTTTTTTTTTT
I  16 [ HHH|PPTTTTTTTTTTTTTTTT
T  15 [ HHH|PPPTTTTTTTTTTTTTTT
   14 [ HHH|PPPPTTTTTTTTTTTTTT
O  13 [ HHH|PPPPPTTTTTTTTTTTTT
R  12 [ HHH|PPPPPPTTTTTTTTTTTT
D  11 [ HHH|PPPPPPPTTTTTTTTTTT
I  10 [ HHH|PPPPPPPPTTTTTTTTTT
N   9 [ HHH|PPPPPPPPPTTTTTTTTT
A   8 [ HHH|PPPPPPPPPPTTTTTTTT
L   7 [ HHH|PPPPPPPPPPPTTTTTTT
    6 [ HHH|PPPPPPPPPPPPTTTTTT
V   5 [ HHH|PPPPPPPPPPPPPTTTTT
A   4 [ HHH|PPPPPPPPPPPPPPTTTT
L   3 [ HHH|PPPPPPPPPPPPPPPTTT
U   2 [ HHH|PPPPPPPPPPPPPPPPTT
E   1 [ HHH|PPPPPPPPPPPPPPPPPP
       =====================
        abc|defghijklmnopqrst
UNIT BY DESCENDING MARGINAL VALUE
```

Each ordinal increment represents a marginal value increment. Symbols H, P, and T represent Hoard, Present and Time value increments respectively. Hoarded value is the present value of a unit not lent. Present value is that of a lent unit had it not been lent. Time value is the expected net value (principal + interest) of the lent unit over a period of time at the market interest rate for that period.

Each vertical bar on the horizontal axis represents one monetary unit, yet each unit has a different marginal value to the owner, as a consequence of marginal utility[1]. This value is expressed on the vertical axis as bar height. One should not conflate value with price. The value of each owned unit increases as the hoard decreases, and therefore the net

Reference

[1] https://en.wikipedia.org/wiki/Marginal_utility

value of the same interest rate (price for money), decreases as the hoard decreases, until it becomes negative (where no more is lent).

The individual's time preference is demonstrated by his valuation between marginal units "c" (the next unit to potentially be lent) and "d" (the last unit lent). The former's present value[1] is higher than can be offset by its potential time value[2], so it is not lent. The latter's present value is not, so it is lent. If the market interest rate rises such that the increase in return on lending "c" exceeds the cardinal value increment of "b" (i.e. chart cell "b19") then "c" will be lent. If the market interest rate falls such that the decrease in return on "d" exceeds "c18" then the loan of "d" will be liquidated.

Total savings is 20 units (units "a" through "t"). Total hoarding is 3 units ("a" through "c"). Total lending is 17 units ("d" through "t"). The individual's capital ratio is therefore 3/17 (~17.65%), represented on the chart as a vertical line between units "c" and "d". The opportunity cost[3] of the hoard is 3 units x the market interest rate. The return on the lending is 17 units x the market interest rate.

It is important to note that since value is subjective[4], only the individual's valuation of the amount of interest is meaningful in this context. The market rate of interest raises his ordinal valuation of the units lent to between "18" and "19". The chart therefore represents market interest as a horizontal line between those increments.

Only the choice to lend or not lend expresses time preference. Depreciation occurs in what is hoarded, not in what is lent. As shown in the Depreciation Principle[5], hoarding is consumption. The common perception that a trading from "producer" to "consumer"

Reference

[1] https://en.wikipedia.org/wiki/Present_value
[2] https://en.wikipedia.org/wiki/Time_value_of_money
[3] https://en.wikipedia.org/wiki/Opportunity_cost
[4] https://en.wikipedia.org/wiki/Subjective_theory_of_value
[5] Chapter: Depreciation Principle

constitutes consumption is a clear error. One can decrease his rate of depreciation and thereby make his hoard last longer, **but to be reflected as time preference one must change his rate of lending.**

Notice that, relative to the previous chart, a decrease in the interest rate by the value of the 18th ordinal increment implies that one less unit is lent.

```
              Individual Capital Ratio (time preference)
                 |
                 |
    21 [         |
    20 [ H       |
    19 [ HH      |
    18 [ HHH     |
 U ---[-----+-------------------- Market Interest (time price)
 N 17 [ HHHH|TTTTTTTTTTTTTTTTT
 I 16 [ HHHH|PTTTTTTTTTTTTTTTT
 T 15 [ HHHH|PPTTTTTTTTTTTTTTT
   14 [ HHHH|PPPTTTTTTTTTTTTTT
 O 13 [ HHHH|PPPPTTTTTTTTTTTTT
 R 12 [ HHHH|PPPPPTTTTTTTTTTTT
 D 11 [ HHHH|PPPPPPTTTTTTTTTTT
 I 10 [ HHHH|PPPPPPPTTTTTTTTTT
 N  9 [ HHHH|PPPPPPPPTTTTTTTTT
 A  8 [ HHHH|PPPPPPPPPTTTTTTTT
 L  7 [ HHHH|PPPPPPPPPPTTTTTTT
    6 [ HHHH|PPPPPPPPPPPTTTTTT
 V  5 [ HHHH|PPPPPPPPPPPPTTTTT
 A  4 [ HHHH|PPPPPPPPPPPPPTTTT
 L  3 [ HHHH|PPPPPPPPPPPPPPTTT
 U  2 [ HHHH|PPPPPPPPPPPPPPPTT
 E  1 [ HHHH|PPPPPPPPPPPPPPPPP
      ========================
         abcd|efghijklmnopqrst
 UNIT BY DESCENDING MARGINAL VALUE
```

This holds at every increment down to the level of interest in which the individual does not lend.

```
                        Individual Capital Ratio (time preference)
                        |
                        |
    21 [                |
    20 [ H              |
    19 [ HH             |
U   18 [ HHH            |
N   17 [ HHHH           |
I   16 [ HHHHH          |
T   15 [ HHHHHH         |
    14 [ HHHHHHH        |
O   13 [ HHHHHHHH       |
R   12 [ HHHHHHHHH      |
D   11 [ HHHHHHHHHH     |
I   10 [ HHHHHHHHHHH    |
N    9 [ HHHHHHHHHHHH   |
A    8 [ HHHHHHHHHHHHH  |
L    7 [ HHHHHHHHHHHHHH |
     6 [ HHHHHHHHHHHHHHH    |
V    5 [ HHHHHHHHHHHHHHHH   |
A    4 [ HHHHHHHHHHHHHHHHH  |
L    3 [ HHHHHHHHHHHHHHHHHH |
U    2 [ HHHHHHHHHHHHHHHHHHH |
E    1 [ HHHHHHHHHHHHHHHHHHHH|
    ---[--------------------+---- Market Interest (time price)
       ========================
         abcdefghijklmnopqrst|
UNIT BY DESCENDING MARGINAL VALUE
```

Similarly this relation holds to the point where the individual lends all of his capital.

```
          Individual Capital Ratio (time preference)
          |
          |
   ---[-+------------------------ Market Interest (time price)
   21 [ |TTTTTTTTTTTTTTTTTTTTT
   20 [ |PTTTTTTTTTTTTTTTTTTTT
   19 [ |PPTTTTTTTTTTTTTTTTTTT
U  18 [ |PPPTTTTTTTTTTTTTTTTTT
N  17 [ |PPPPTTTTTTTTTTTTTTTTT
I  16 [ |PPPPPTTTTTTTTTTTTTTTT
T  15 [ |PPPPPPTTTTTTTTTTTTTTT
   14 [ |PPPPPPPTTTTTTTTTTTTTT
O  13 [ |PPPPPPPPTTTTTTTTTTTTT
R  12 [ |PPPPPPPPPTTTTTTTTTTTT
D  11 [ |PPPPPPPPPPTTTTTTTTTTT
I  10 [ |PPPPPPPPPPPTTTTTTTTTT
N   9 [ |PPPPPPPPPPPPTTTTTTTTT
A   8 [ |PPPPPPPPPPPPPTTTTTTTT
L   7 [ |PPPPPPPPPPPPPPTTTTTTT
    6 [ |PPPPPPPPPPPPPPPTTTTTT
V   5 [ |PPPPPPPPPPPPPPPPTTTTT
A   4 [ |PPPPPPPPPPPPPPPPPTTTT
L   3 [ |PPPPPPPPPPPPPPPPPPTTT
U   2 [ |PPPPPPPPPPPPPPPPPPPPT
E   1 [ |PPPPPPPPPPPPPPPPPPPPP
      ==========================
          |abcdefghijklmnopqrst
UNIT BY DESCENDING MARGINAL VALUE
```

Speculative Consumption

Catallactics[1] defines two categories of capital use, consumption, and production. Products are produced and consumed. Production, or the creation of products, requires time and therefore saved capital (investment). Consumption also requires time, and therefore saved capital (hoard).

Human energy can be expended in leisure or labor[2], where the depreciation of stored human energy is a factor (cost) of production. In either case conversion of this potential energy[3] to work4[4] is a consumption of stored capital. Labor may produce food and the person may immediately eat it. This is an absolute subsistence economy[5], where the only savings is potential energy stored in one's body. The product of labor, time and nature-given[6] factors is continuously consumed, either in production (e.g. picking berries) or leisure (e.g. sleep). This is sometimes referred to as living "hand to mouth." The property saved in this process is the person's own body. A child begins life with potential energy gifted by its mother.

Savings is therefore the only source of both production and leisure. The question then arises, to which is the savings applied? Even in the case of food that has been digested, the question remains. Capital applied to production is traded for the ownership of what is eventually produced. This ownership of a future good is called a "savings-investment" (or simply "investment"). Capital not applied to production is called a "savings-hoard" (or

Reference

[1] https://en.wikipedia.org/wiki/Catallactics
[2] https://mises.org/library/man-economy-and-state-power-and-market/html/p/926
[3] https://en.wikipedia.org/wiki/Potential_energy
[4] https://en.wikipedia.org/wiki/Potential_energy#Work_and_potential_energy
[5] https://en.wikipedia.org/wiki/Subsistence_economy
[6] https://mises.org/library/man-economy-and-state-power-and-market/html/p/939

simply "hoard"). Savings is the sum of one's hoarded *and* invested capital. The process of applying hoarded capital to investment or leisure is called "dishoarding"[1].

> After he sells his services, he acquires his money income from production, thereby adding to his money stock. He then allocates this income between consumption and savings-investment, and we are assuming no hoarding or dishoarding.
>
> *Murray Rothbard: Man, Economy and State*

Catallactics deals with human *action*, explicitly rejecting analysis of human *thoughts*. Thoughts are subjective, expressed objectively only in the action of a trade. This principle is embodied in the theory of subjective value[2]. As a necessary factor of both production and leisure, time is *assumed* to have objective value. There is no expression of whether one's savings is to be used in production or leisure until it is dishoarded. One may prefer savings for production, but then oversleep, consuming the savings in leisure. Similarly one may generally prefer apples, but trade an apple for an orange. The only objective expression of a preference is a trade, including the trade of savings for consumption by production or leisure. As not applied to production, hoarded capital is called "unproductive", just as is a person not engaged in production.

Hoarding is a necessary consequence of uncertainty. As uncertainty rises people tend to increase their level of hoarding, either restricting leisure or production. This allows their hoarded capital to be applied to either in the future. Yet unproductive capital incurs time costs. Time is objectively valuable. The opportunity to use the capital in production has been traded for increased certainty. This is the opportunity cost[3] of certainty, an expense. Both productive and unproductive uses of capital trade opportunity for

Reference

[1] https://mises.org/library/man-economy-and-state-power-and-market/html/p/992
[2] https://en.wikipedia.org/wiki/Subjective_theory_of_value
[3] https://en.wikipedia.org/wiki/Opportunity_cost

certainty. The hoard is referred to as "liquidity" and is necessary only due to the fact of uncertainty[1].

As shown in Savings Relation[2], the ratio of savings hoarded to that invested is an expression of human time preference[3]. As with all valuations, that of certainty relative to opportunity cost is subjective. While time has objective utility (i.e. more time is worth more than less), the value remains relative and subjective. Yet, as with all valuations, the consequence is an objective price for capital over time, expressed by exchange and referred to as the rate of interest. Interest is both the return on capital and the cost of capital. Opportunity cost is the loss of productive gain that arises from hoarding capital, measured by the rate of interest.

A hoard represents the subjective valuation that it is worth more over time than the opportunity cost that it represents over that time. This is called "speculation". It is the expression of a preference for owning a good over parting with it, with its cost measured by interest foregone. The opportunity to invest the hoard over the time hoarded is lost forever. In other words, the act of not investing capital is the consumption of capital. With all capital hoarded, there is no production of new capital and eventually all capital is consumed.

How the speculation is "justified" is not relevant to this distinction, as value is subjective. Yet some level of hoarding is necessary due to the fact of uncertainty (i.e. of the future). A preference for capital in the present, as opposed to more in the future, is always expressed in hoarding. One may certainly hoard at a level beyond the liquidity intended to offset uncertainty. For example, one may hoard for the entertainment value of games of chance[4]. The opportunity cost in this case is an entertainment expense. One may hoard

Reference

[1] https://mises.org/wire/problem-hoarding
[2] Chapter: Savings Relation
[3] Chapter: Time Preference Fallacy
[4] https://en.wikipedia.org/wiki/Game_of_chance

while timing a sale[1]. The opportunity cost of in this case is called "cash drag". It matters not whether the person anticipates a net gain or realizes one, the hoard necessarily represents an expense – because time has value.

However, time preference is sometimes misinterpreted as a relation between consumption and saving. This is often loosely described as "deferred consumption" or "delayed gratification". Yet as has been shown, hoarding is consumption. The consumption has not been deferred; the gratification has not been delayed. Offsetting uncertainty is gratification (peace of mind), entertainment is gratification (leisure activity), the potential gain on successful market timing is gratification (anticipation of better price). All of these consume capital. The distinction made by the concept of time preference is in the exchange of capital over time in exchange for interest. A speculation makes no such trade.

All of a person's property (savings) is either hoarded or invested. Hoarding erodes that property over time. Cars wear out, food gets converted to energy, furniture wears out, capital decays. Money is no different, it decays in a hoard due to both its carry cost[2] and its opportunity cost. The present value[3] of money is always discounted against its future value. This is described as the "time value of money". By expending the future value, the money hoard is actually depreciating by the amount of the discount over the time hoarded.

As shown in Depreciation Principle[4] the act of purchasing goods is not consumption. There is no actual consumption except to the extent that property depreciates. As such there is no distinction between deferring the purchase of goods and purchasing them. This is just a trade of one type of property for another, both subject to depreciation. Time

Reference

[1] https://en.wikipedia.org/wiki/Market_timing
[2] https://en.wikipedia.org/wiki/Cost_of_carry
[3] https://en.wikipedia.org/wiki/Present_value
[4] Chapter: Depreciation Principle

preference is not a distinction between consumption and saving, it is a distinction between hoarding and investment.

Entrepreneurship necessarily entails speculation and investment. Capital is required for production, and the entrepreneur is speculating on the price of what is to be produced. This speculation on a future good is the unavoidable side effect of producing products with no established price. Entrepreneurship is therefore "speculative production", while depreciation of a present good is "speculative consumption". Given that any future price estimate is subject to error, all investment is to some extent entrepreneurial. Investment is speculative production and hoarding is speculative consumption. This is evident in the fact that, with all capital hoarded, there is no production.

The above discussion makes a distinction between productive and consumptive use of capital, in the context of a single person. In the interest of simplicity we have discussed only leisure consumption (i.e. of a consumer's hoard), avoiding productive consumption (i.e. of a producer's hoard). While a single person may be both consumer and producer, a producer must also consume in production. As the terms thus become overloaded, it is easier to think of a person's investment as being in another person's production business.

The *objective* of a person is leisure while that of a business is production. Both objectives are consumptive in nature, yet consumption in the context of a business is for production, not leisure. Just as any person, a business must determine its ratio of hoard to investment based on time preference. The investments of a business cannot be in its own production, just as those of a person cannot be in his own leisure, as either would be circular. A business acquires assets and depreciates them over time. While these are often colloquially referred to as investments, a business does not pay itself interest. These assets are hoarded capital in the process of consumption, for the objective of production. Its remaining capital is invested in other businesses, such as investment funds or interest-bearing bank accounts. As each person and business hoards a fraction[1] of its capital and invests the remainder, credit expands[2] on money[3] as a function of time preference.

The idea of a person being both consumer and producer raises the categorical question of labor. While all people must consume, most are also producers. A person engaged in salaried labor is a producer. A salaryman[4] invests capital in his person (e.g. education, reputation, food) and invests time without his human capital when his person is away from his objective of leisure. Salary and associated benefits are his return on investment. Due to labor competition, this return seeks the level of interest on his marketable value over the time laboring.

Speculation is a necessary consequence of error inherent in both consumption and investment. Hoarding is consumptive and investing is productive. The economic concept of time preference is specifically the distinction between hoarding and investment. This is evident in the identity relation between time preference and economic interest. **A higher proportion of hoarding to investment reflects a higher time preference and implies less production.**

Reference

[1] Chapter: Full Reserve Fallacy

[2] Chapter: Credit Expansion Fallacy

[3] Chapter: Money Taxonomy

[4] https://en.wikipedia.org/wiki/Salaryman

Subjective Inflation Principle

Free market price inflation[1] is entirely the consequence of personal preferences, and therefore not derivable from anything else.

- Goods prices are determined subjectively. (Subjective Theory of Value[2])
- Time preference determines expansion[3] of credit on money. (Time Preference Axiom[4])
- Creation of money[5] is not price inflationary. (Inflation Principle[6])

This could be more simply obtained from the definition of free market, as entirely the consequence of personal preferences.

Reference

[1] https://en.m.wikipedia.org/wiki/Inflation

[2] https://en.m.wikipedia.org/wiki/Subjective_theory_of_value

[3] Chapter: Credit Expansion Fallacy

[4] Chapter: Time Preference Fallacy

[5] Chapter: Money Taxonomy

[6] Chapter: Inflation Principle

Time Preference Fallacy

There is a theory that lower time preference[1] is better than higher, as it results in greater production and therefore greater wealth. This is a reversal of cause and effect.

Time preference is the economic axiom[2] that states people prefer a "present good" over the same "future good". As a conflict with subjective value[3], this idea cannot be proven. Time is unique in that it is assumed to have inherent value. This assumption is grounded in the observations that people have limited time and that it is a necessary factor of all production.

Value derives from the human perception of utility. A person who trades a car for a horse objectively values the usefulness of owning the horse more than the car. This implies nothing about why one is more valuable to the person than the other, even given the exchange. The value placed on one good over another is a preference[4]. It cannot be shown that a person will express a preference for any good, even his own life. The reason for a preference is not provable in rational economic theory[5], with one exception – the effect of wealth on time preference.

Diminishing marginal utility[6] implies that each additional unit of a good accumulated by a person has a lower utility to the person than the previous. This implies that, for a given interest rate, increasing wealth implies an increasing willingness to lend. This is

Reference

[1] https://en.m.wikipedia.org/wiki/Time_preference

[2] https://en.m.wikipedia.org/wiki/Axiom

[3] https://en.m.wikipedia.org/wiki/Subjective_theory_of_value

[4] https://en.wikipedia.org/wiki/Preference#Economics

[5] https://en.wikipedia.org/wiki/Catallactics

[6] https://en.m.wikipedia.org/wiki/Marginal_utility

the expression of falling time preference, and is subsequently reflected in a falling interest rate due to the increased supply of capital competing for loans.

The economic rate of interest is merely a reflection of time preference. While anything can affect a person's time preference, only a change to wealth implies a necessary change. A higher interest rate implies a greater willingness for a person of a given time preference to lend. It would be an error however to assume that higher interest rates increase time preference. It is a similar error to assume that a person will be wealthier if he lowers his time preference. These are both reversals of cause and effect. As such the theory is invalid.

Infinite time preference implies no lending and therefore no production. Zero time preference implies no consumption of what is produced. Given that production exists only to satisfy eventual consumption, zero time preference also implies no production, as there is no value attributable to the consumption of products. Therefore lowest time preference is not inherently more productive. As such the theory is invalid. Time preference is a balance between consumption and production.

A person's wealth increases only to the extent that he is more able to satisfy his preferences, including those for present and deferred consumption. States employ fiscal and monetary stimulus[1] in an attempt to increase consumption or production respectively. Yet this comes at the cost of taxation. The outcome is the shifting of capital allocation decisions from the market to the state, resulting in capital wasted on unconsumed (glut) or unavailable (shortage) products. This implies people are less able to *satisfy* preferences. However it implies no change to the preferences that they hold, except as tax diminishes their wealth or subsidy increases it.

Reference

[1] https://en.m.wikipedia.org/wiki/Stimulus_(economics)

Economics does not make value judgments, it infers their necessary consequence. The theory presumes a morality, which can be assumed but must be objective. Aggression differentiates the free market from market intervention, such as by the state. However, even if one accepts nonaggression[1] as the moral divide, no moral distinction between higher and lower time preference exists. There is no ratio of consumption to production that implies aggression, it remains subjective despite being affected by wealth. As such the theory is invalid.

It can be enlightening to consider the subjectivity of value in terms of sexual preference.

```
{ X, Y }
{ X->X, Y->Y }
{ X->X|Y, Y->X|Y }
{ X->Y, Y->X }
```

One might consider this list ordered in terms of increasing production (i.e. producing more humans). Many states attempt to reduce the expression of sexual preference to the set { X->Y, Y->X }. Both outright criminalization[2] of expression and explicit financial incentive[3] for it are employed to this end. This has a discernible impact on expression of sexual preference but cannot be said to have any impact on the preference itself.

Similarly it should be clear that an increase in production is not objectively good. People doing what they prefer is the moral good, again assuming the moral principle of nonaggression. Even if we assume all people prefer continuation of the species[4], this implies no effect on individual sexual preferences.

Reference

[1] https://en.m.wikipedia.org/wiki/Non-aggression_principle

[2] https://en.m.wikipedia.org/wiki/LGBT_rights_by_country_or_territory

[3] https://en.m.wikipedia.org/wiki/Marriage_promotion

[4] https://futurism.com/in-order-to-ensure-human-survival-we-must-become-a-multi-planetary-species

A related theory states that people can demonstrate lower time preference by hoarding more bitcoin. An increased level of hoarding at the expense of lending implies *higher* time preference. An increased level of hoarding at the expense of consumption seems to imply a lower time preference, since consumption appears deferred. Yet a hoard represents only the liquidity required for consumption.

As a game of chance[1], any speculation is consumption of the cost of "playing", supported by its required liquidity. This cost is, at a minimum, the opportunity cost[2] of not lending the amount (i.e. interest). Despite the fact that the game, like all consumption, requires time, the expressed preference is to play the game, not to capture time value. As such this theory is also invalid.

There is a related theory that time preference is expressed by deferred consumption – when a person accumulates savings vs. consuming those savings. As shown in Speculative Consumption[3] this misrepresents all savings as implied investment. Savings is a general term encompassing both a person's hoard and investment.

Savings is the *source* of all investment, but only actual investment expresses time preference. A hoard can certainly change in marketable value. **But considering a greater hoard an expression of lower time preference is a common colloquial misinterpretation of the economic meaning of the term.** This reverses its meaning, leading to such conclusions such as full hoarding expresses zero time preference. Yet with full hoarding interest rates are infinite, and infinite interest reflects infinite time preference. This direct contradiction exposes the fact that the meaning of the term time preference has been reversed, invalidating the theory.

Reference

[1] https://en.wikipedia.org/wiki/Game_of_chance
[2] https://en.m.wikipedia.org/wiki/Opportunity_cost
[3] Chapter: Speculative Consumption

MONEY

Collectible Tautology

In attempting to apply the Regression Theorem[1] to Bitcoin one may postulate that Bitcoin began as a "collectible", arising from interest by monetary theorists. The collectible obtained original use value[2] due to their personal preferences. It was then bartered[3] as a consequence of this value, transitioning to a medium of exchange[4] based on the memory of barter value.

This appears consistent with the theorem[5], which argues that all money[6] *must* originate from a commodity[7] that obtains barter and then monetary exchange value. Yet if commodity value can arise from potential as money then the theorem is tautological[8], implying nothing more than money is money.

> Now, the regression theorem aims at interpreting the first emergence of a monetary demand for a good which previously had been demanded exclusively for industrial purposes as influenced by the exchange value that was ascribed to it at this moment on account of its nonmonetary services only.
>
> *Ludwig von Mises: Human Action*

The postulate takes advantage of colloquial ambiguity in the word "commodity", despite the explicit reference to "industrial" use value in the theorem itself. **If anything can be a**

Reference

[1] Chapter: Regression Fallacy

[2] https://en.m.wikipedia.org/wiki/Use_value

[3] https://en.m.wikipedia.org/wiki/Barter

[4] https://en.m.wikipedia.org/wiki/Medium_of_exchange

[5] https://mises.org/library/human-action-0/html/pp/778

[6] Chapter: Money Taxonomy

[7] https://en.m.wikipedia.org/wiki/Commodity

[8] https://en.m.wikipedia.org/wiki/Tautology_(logic)

commodity then the Regression Theorem would imply, contrary to its assertion, that anything can be money.

> In economics, a commodity is an economic good or service that has full or substantial fungibility: that is, the market treats instances of the good as equivalent or nearly so with no regard to who produced them. [...]
>
> Most commodities are raw materials, basic resources, agricultural, or mining products, such as iron ore, sugar, or grains like rice and wheat. Commodities can also be mass-produced unspecialized products such as chemicals and computer memory.
>
> *Wikipedia: Commodity*

The Regression Theorem uses "commodity" to distinguish money from something with no original use value. If it intends that *anything* is a commodity, it is tautological, and otherwise the postulate is a misrepresentation of the theorem.

Debt Loop Fallacy

There is a theory that there is no actual money[1] in modern state systems of currency[2]. Instead what is commonly referred to as "fiat" money is actually a money substitute[3] (e.g. a legally enforceable claim for money). A money substitute is an obligation to redeem the substitute for the borrowed money that it represents, so even definitionally this presents a problem – the basis of the term "loop". The theory relies on the observation that the state both issues the currency and accepts it, implying an obligation to do so, such as in the cancellation of debt to the state (e.g. taxes). As such at issuance the claim is a credit against future tax settlement, etc. (i.e. the actual money).

Yet money substitutes are claims to a definite amount of money[4], as otherwise they are not fungible. The amount of tax liability represented by a $100 note, in payment of $100 of tax, is defined in terms of itself (i.e. the logical error of circular reasoning[5]) . The amount it offsets is whatever the state is willing to trade for it. This would be the case for any money, including 100 ounces of gold or 100 units of fiat. **Money does not represent any amount of another good, it represents whatever it can be traded for.**

The state incurs no debt in declaring that it will accept a money, whether it be gold or fiat. Similarly a business that declares that it will take a particular money incurs no debt by doing so. The debt of representative money[6] (a form of money substitute) such as a gold certificate[7], is expressed in the trade of the gold for the certificate-holder's claim against it. Issuance of the money does not change this fact. The state or a business can

Reference

[1] Chapter: Money Taxonomy
[2] https://en.wikipedia.org/wiki/Currency
[3] https://wiki.mises.org/wiki/Money_substitutes
[4] https://wiki.mises.org/wiki/Money_substitutes#Nature
[5] https://en.wikipedia.org/wiki/Circular_reasoning
[6] https://en.wikipedia.org/wiki/Representative_money
[7] https://en.wikipedia.org/wiki/Gold_certificate

certainly issue gold in trade without the gold being considered a debt. State fiat enjoys monopoly protection[1] on issuance, guaranteeing the state a profit[2] from doing so. But this is not relevant to the question of whether the fiat is money or debt.

No money has intrinsic value. Fiat is distinguished from commodity money, such as gold, only by the presumption of no use value[3]. But given that value is subjective[4], this is not a material distinction. Nor is it an actual one, as paper money can be burned for heat. If the state mined, minted and accepted gold or bitcoin, the theory would have to consider units of gold and bitcoin debt under the same criteria it applies to fiat.

The theory represents a misunderstanding of the nature of money substitutes. A claim cannot be a claim for itself. In such a scenario, the claim would settle[5] itself. In other words, if $100 was a claim for $100 worth of anything, holding the claim is satisfaction of the claim. It would not be a claim at all, it would be money. As such the theory is invalid.

The transition from claim to fiat happens when representative money is abrogated by its issuer. The U.S. Dollar was monetized in 1934[6] when its redeemability was cancelled. People were compelled to exchange redeemable dollars for irredeemable dollars. To the extent that formerly-redeemable dollars remain in circulation, as many still do, they are converted when encountered by the Federal Reserve[7]. The retention of the phrase "Federal Reserve Note" on the irredeemable Dollar is anachronistic.

Reference

[1] https://en.wikipedia.org/wiki/Counterfeit
[2] https://en.wikipedia.org/wiki/Seigniorage
[3] https://en.wikipedia.org/wiki/Use_value
[4] https://en.wikipedia.org/wiki/Subjective_theory_of_value
[5] https://en.wikipedia.org/wiki/Clearing_(finance)
[6] https://en.wikipedia.org/wiki/Gold_Reserve_Act
[7] https://en.wikipedia.org/wiki/Federal_Reserve

All money implies money substitutes, as a consequence of lending[1]. We can classify four hypothetical scenarios for money substitutes in terms of debt regression, where each step in the regression is a promissory note[2].

- no regression (money)
- single regression (representative money)
- finite regression (money substitute)
- infinite regression (impossible money)

A note may be a claim for another type of claim, but not for itself (i.e. whatever it can be traded for). Otherwise there is no actual regression and the supposed claim *is* money. This holds in the case where the claim is directly or indirectly entirely circular, as implied by the term "loop", as the note settles itself. So the term "debt loop" is simply another description for "money". Examples include Gold, Bitcoin, and the irredeemable (modern) U.S. Dollar.

A direct claim (single regression) for money is a representative money, though this term is generally reserved for a tangible note that represents a commodity money[3]. The note directly represents money. The redeemable U.S. Dollar was a representative money.

An indirect claim represents any finite progression of claims against others. When all claims are settled, the money is held by its rightful owner with all claims closed out, and any circular claims fully netted[4]. Note that if the claims are fully circular there is nothing to settle (i.e. the claim is money).

Reference

[1] Chapter: Credit Expansion Fallacy

[2] https://en.wikipedia.org/wiki/Promissory_note

[3] https://en.wikipedia.org/wiki/Commodity_money

[4] https://en.wikipedia.org/wiki/Set-off_(law)#Close_out_netting

An infinite regression of claims cannot exist[1]. Consider a hypothetical note issued by the state treasury with redeemability in terms of offsetting state tax liability.

- $1 settles the tax liability on $10 of income.
- $10 settles the tax liability on $100 of income.
- $100 settles the tax liability on $1000 of income.
- and so on...

While the note does not represent itself, its regression is infinite. A claim can only be made against a finite number of other claims. In this case any such instrument is not actually a note and could only trade as money.

Reference

[1] https://en.wikipedia.org/wiki/Turtles_all_the_way_down

Ideal Money Fallacy

It has been proposed[1] that the existence of an international non-political (i.e. objective) "value index" will result in people compelling states to "value target" their monies against the index, thereby eliminating price inflation[2]. It has also been suggested that Bitcoin is such an index and will precipitate this scenario.

The leverage envisioned is the option to leave certain state monies for others. The movement is from monies of higher inflation to lower, based on comparison with the index. The consequence is that states must increasingly target their individual rates of price inflation to the index. This result is state monies "asymptotically" approaching the condition of Ideal Money[3] represented by the index.

Ideal Money is state money with a zero rate of price inflation:

> ...there is no ideal rate of inflation that should be selected and chosen as the target but rather that the ideal concept would necessarily be that of a zero rate for what is called inflation.
>
> *John F. Nash Jr.: Ideal Money and Asymptotically Ideal Money*

Expression of the theory is both varied and limited (proof is left to the reader). However the above summary expresses all essential elements. Given these limitations it can be helpful to start with generous assumptions. Let us assume that a money can express objective value (see subjective theory of value[4]), that Bitcoin is such a money, and that people generally have the ability to compare the value of Bitcoin to other major state monies. Let us also assume that, despite the apparent contradiction, people will both

Reference

[1] http://sites.stat.psu.edu/~gjb6/nash/money.pdf

[2] https://en.wikipedia.org/wiki/Inflation

[3] https://en.wikipedia.org/wiki/Ideal_money

[4] https://en.wikipedia.org/wiki/Subjective_theory_of_value

generally use Bitcoin in trade (the source of the index) *and* will prefer to use state monies (a necessary premise).

If we also assume that people are free from legal tender laws[1], and their use of competing currencies does succeed in compelling states to "value target" Bitcoin, seigniorage6[2] will be eliminated. However, as shown in Stability Property[3], the purpose of state money (fiat[4]) is to collect seigniorage, which is a tax. In other words, Ideal Money is a tax collection system that collects no tax. Granting the above assumptions, Ideal Money is the obsolescence of state money. **The proposal fails to consider the reason that fiat exists in the first place.**

Reconsider now the assumptions. Fiat requires the existence of legal tender laws and as such Gresham's Law[5] (first penned by Nicole Oresme[6] in *De origine, natura, jure et mutationibus monetarum* c. 1360) always governs fiat:

> These examples show that, in the absence of effective legal tender laws, Gresham's Law works in reverse. If given the choice of what money to accept, people will transact with money they believe to be of highest long-term value. However, if not given the choice, and required to accept all money, good and bad, they will tend to keep the money of greater perceived value in their possession, and pass on the bad money to someone else. In short, in the absence of legal tender laws, the seller will not accept anything but money of certain value (good money), while the existence of legal tender laws will cause the buyer to offer only money with the lowest commodity value (bad money) as the creditor must accept such money at face value.
>
> *Wikipedia: Gresham's Law*

Reference

[1] https://en.wikipedia.org/wiki/Legal_tender

[2] https://en.wikipedia.org/wiki/Seigniorage

[3] Chapter: Stability Property

[4] https://en.wikipedia.org/wiki/Fiat_money

[5] https://en.wikipedia.org/wiki/Gresham%27s_law

[6] https://en.wikipedia.org/wiki/Nicole_Oresme

The proposal incorrectly assumes that Thiers' Law[1] governs. If this were the case people would not use fiat. It also ignores the existence of foreign exchange controls[2], which exist specifically to prevent capital flight[3]. Such controls strengthen as capital flight accelerates, in order to preserve tax revenue. Finally, such controls materially limit price discovery in the index, making it less useful than the envisioned reference.

The proposal offers no rational explanation for how people will become able to move between state monies in the face of such controls. It assumes that people will better recognize the tax, due to the presence of the index and their ability to compare against it, and therefore will more effectively control the state's appetite for the tax. Given the near universal use of gold as a comparably objective index prior to the evolution of global fiat, it is not clear how fiat ever took hold if we can assume people will react to it in this manner.

There is an argument that Bitcoin is an objective index whereas gold is not. This is based on the inflationary supply of gold in contrast to the fixed supply of Bitcoin. This assumes that monetary inflation implies an unstable money whereas fixed supply implies a stable money. As shown in Stability Property, both monies are stable. The argument fails to acknowledge that value, as indicated by the index, is a consequence of both supply and demand. Gold demand is stabilized by inflation and Bitcoin's demand is stabilized by fees.

The theory is therefore invalid. Either fiat will cease to exist or it will collect tax. States only surrender this tax under extreme duress and in such cases only briefly. If anything the "ideal money" will be Bitcoin, and it will not trade freely with state monies (to the extent they remain).

Reference

[1] https://en.wikipedia.org/wiki/Gresham%27s_law#Reverse_of_Gresham's_law_(Thiers'_law)
[2] https://en.wikipedia.org/wiki/Foreign_exchange_controls
[3] https://en.wikipedia.org/wiki/Capital_flight

Inflation Fallacy

Bitcoin consensus rules create a period of monetary inflation[1]. There is a theory that this causes the money to lose purchasing power[2]. As shown in Inflation Principle[3], **no change in purchasing power is implied by supply increase of a market money**. The theory is therefore invalid.

The fact that Bitcoin is not price inflationary implies that owners do not "subsidize" mining. The capital consumed by miners is their own (investment), the money created is their own product, and the return on investment (interest) is a consequence of the increase in demand that they alone provide – offsetting the opportunity cost[4] of deploying their own capital over time.

Reference

[1] https://en.wikipedia.org/wiki/Monetary_inflation

[2] https://en.wikipedia.org/wiki/Purchasing_power

[3] Chapter: Inflation Principle

[4] https://en.m.wikipedia.org/wiki/Opportunity_cost

Money Taxonomy

Fiat money does not have use value[1]. It has utility as a money only to the extent that people are willing to trade for it. These people may and often do include an issuing state, though this is not a distinguishing characteristic. The name derives from the fact that it is decreed to exist ("dixitque Deus fiat lux et facta est lux"[2]) as money. However such a declaration is also not a distinguishing characteristic. **Fiat is simply money without use value.** Money with use value is referred to as commodity money[3].

While value is subjective[4], making it impossible to determine use value in practice, the classification itself is clear. Paper money can be burned for heat, but this is typically not considered a material use value. Bitcoin can be used for timestamping[5], but this is also not typically considered a material use value. Gold, silver, copper, and other coinage is generally considered to have material use value. When a commodity money's face value becomes less than its commodity value, it has transitioned to a commodity[6] and is melted or hoarded[7].

A money substitute[8] is a contractual claim[9] to a definite amount of money, redeemable on demand. As such a money substitute represents a "future good" while money is a "present good". Fiat is not a money substitute[10] because it is not redeemable for any

Reference

[1] https://en.wikipedia.org/wiki/Use_value

[2] https://en.wikipedia.org/wiki/Let_there_be_light#Origin_and_etymology

[3] https://en.wikipedia.org/wiki/Commodity_money

[4] https://en.wikipedia.org/wiki/Subjective_theory_of_value

[5] https://en.wikipedia.org/wiki/Trusted_timestamping

[6] https://en.wikipedia.org/wiki/Venezuelan_bol%C3%ADvar#Bol%C3%ADvar_fuerte_2

[7] https://en.wikipedia.org/wiki/Gresham%27s_law

[8] https://wiki.mises.org/wiki/Money_substitutes

[9] https://financial-dictionary.thefreedictionary.com/Contractual+Claim

[10] Chapter: Debt Loop Fallacy

definite amount of money, it is the money itself. Debt is often securitized[1] and guaranteed by the lender as a money substitute, known as a banknote[2]. Given that value is subjective, it is also not possible to distinguish whether a person values the redemption, or the claim itself, but the assumption is generally that the redemption is valued, not the document it is written on. When a money substitute is abrogated yet still trades it has transitioned to fiat[3].

Representative money[4] is often misinterpreted as a present good, yet because it is a claim (to what it represents), it is a money substitute. The gold-backed U.S. Dollar was a money substitute and the modern U.S. Dollar is fiat. Account-based U.S. Dollars are electronic money substitutes[5], just as are all custodial Bitcoin accounts and trade in unconfirmed transactions. These are promises to redeem in dollars or bitcoin respectively.

The dollars that one can hold in one's hand are fiat, just as are the bitcoin that one can spend with one's private keys. As such the term "fiat" alone does not distinguish between the Dollar and Bitcoin. *However this distinction was never required before the existence of Bitcoin.* Market monies without use value were presumed not to be possible[6]. However there is a material distinction between these two types of money, neither of which have use value. This begs for a new differentiating term.

Reference

[1] https://en.wikipedia.org/wiki/Securitization
[2] https://en.wikipedia.org/wiki/Banknote
[3] https://en.wikipedia.org/wiki/Gold_certificate
[4] https://en.wikipedia.org/wiki/Representative_money
[5] https://www.investopedia.com/terms/e/electronic-money.asp
[6] Chapter: Regression Fallacy

The Dollar (as all state fiat) differs from Bitcoin in that it depends on monopoly protection[1] for production. It is this prohibition of market competition that allows the state to limit supply and therefore extract seigniorage[2].

> monopoly is a grant of special privilege by the State, reserving a certain area of production to one particular individual or group
>
> *Murray Rothbard: Man, Economy and State*

The monopoly on production of state fiat is created by anti-counterfeit[3] statute. A unit of the money is considered invalid unless produced by an authorized agent[4] of the state. This is distinct from Bitcoin, as it is produced by market competition and counterfeit is precluded by agreement on a public ledger. Money secured against counterfeit by statute may then reasonably be referred to as "monopoly money" (not to be confused with Monopoly Money[5]), and Bitcoin as "market money". When the face value of fiat is reduced to its production cost it has transitioned to market money[6].

Commodity money is also market money, as it does not rely on monopoly privilege to restrict its supply. If commodity money supply is too great, it ceases to be a useful money due to the lack of portability. The distinction between commodity money and Bitcoin is obtained from cryptodynamic principles[7]. Commodity money supply is controlled through market competition to supply it, as a consequence of its market demand. It is not fiat given the presumption of use value.

Reference

[1] https://mises.org/library/man-economy-and-state-power-and-market/html/pp/1054

[2] https://en.wikipedia.org/wiki/Seigniorage

[3] https://en.wikipedia.org/wiki/Counterfeit_money

[4] https://www.moneyfactory.gov

[5] https://monopoly.fandom.com/wiki/Monopoly_Money

[6] https://en.wikipedia.org/wiki/Zimbabwean_dollar

[7] Chapter: Cryptodynamic Principles

Both money and money substitutes constitute currency[1]. Money is sometimes referred to as base money. All monies are subject to lending and therefore necessarily credit expansion[2] (i.e. into money substitutes) and its corresponding fractional reservation[3].

Reference

[1] https://en.wikipedia.org/wiki/Currency

[2] Chapter: Credit Expansion Fallacy

[3] Chapter: Reserve Definition

The following table offers examples of each of the aforementioned classifications.

- currency

  - money [*present*]

    - commodity [*use value*]

      monopoly

      U.S. Dollar Coin

      market

      Bullion

    - fiat [*no use value*]

      monopoly

      U.S. Dollar Bill

      market

      Bitcoin

  - money substitute [*future*]

    - electronic [*intangible*]

      account

      Visa

    - representative [*tangible*]

      banknote

      U.S. Silver Certificate

Regression Fallacy

The Regression Theorem[1] relies on the assumption that the first people to value something as a money[2] must do so based on a memory of its prior use value[3], with the thing eventually obtaining barter[4] utility and finally monetary value[5].

> No good can be employed for the function of a medium of exchange which at the very beginning of its use for this purpose did not have exchange value on account of other employments.
>
> *Ludwig von Mises: Human Action*

Notice that the theory does not merely attempt to explain the origin of the money concept, but of *anything that can be a money*. In other words, if a good does not follow this progression, it is not money.

The theorem contradicts the subjective theory of value[6] upon which it relies. Value is subjective, which implies it can be based on anything, even if objectively that basis appears irrational.

The theorem fails to terminate its regression by not explaining how a person comes to value something for its original utility. One must assume (not remember) something will be useful if nobody has ever attempted to use it. This assumption of utility is the first

Reference

[1] https://wiki.mises.org/wiki/Regression_theorem

[2] Chapter: Money Taxonomy

[3] https://en.m.wikipedia.org/wiki/Use_value

[4] https://en.m.wikipedia.org/wiki/Barter

[5] https://mises.org/library/human-action-0/html/pp/778

[6] https://en.m.wikipedia.org/wiki/Subjective_theory_of_value

valuation, which remains subjective. The first valuation of a thing, like all after, can be for any reason, including its use as a money[1].

Given a pre-existing concept of money, it has been suggested[2] that anticipation of being a money is sufficient to satisfy the theorem. In other words the money does not need to follow the progression in actual practice. In this case, given a pre-existing concept of money, anything can begin as money. This interpretation renders the theorem tautological – anything that people value as money can be money. In other words, it reduces to subjective first value.

The theorem is actually based on the *empirical* observation of monetary evolution. Yet the rational economic theory[3] on which it is based, and the theorem itself, explicitly reject empiricism.

> All these statements implied in the regression theorem are enounced apodictically as implied in the apriorism of praxeology. It must happen this way. Nobody can ever succeed in construction a hypothetical case in which things were to occur in a different way.

One of many problems with empirical economics is that new observations can invalidate previous conclusions. Bitcoin has done so to this theorem which purported to be non-empirical. It can clearly be observed that Satoshi intended to create a money[4], for its first use as money.

The idea is a reasonable empirical *theory* on the evolution of the concept of money, but invalid as a rational *theorem* to distinguish money from non-money. Money is

Reference

[1] Chapter: Collectible Tautology

[2] https://mises.org/library/cryptocurrencies-and-wider-regression-theorem

[3] https://en.m.wikipedia.org/wiki/Catallactics

[4] https://bitcoin.org/bitcoin.pdf

distinguished by certain behaviors expressed by people. Concluding that something is a money consists of observing those behaviors, a strictly empirical method.

Reserve Definition

A reserve is the capital a person possesses. It is present capital, as opposed to invested capital. Present capital depreciates[1] and as such represents an ongoing cost to its owner. The ratio of reserved to invested capital is a reflection[2] of the owner's time preference.

Reserve capital intended for the settlement[3] of debts is the settlement medium. For example, where gold is the settlement medium, gold is the reserve capital. A promise for gold, such as a gold certificate[4], is a loan and therefore not a reserve against the debt. If the debt can be settled with gold certificates, then possession of the certificates constitutes reserve.

While holding a certificate as reserve against certificate debt may appear to contradict the definition of reserve as present capital, it does not. As the settlement medium the certificate itself is nothing more than a piece of paper to the person holding it in reserve. The terms it carries are to be passed to the certificate's issuer. No costs or gains in settling the certificate are experienced by the person holding it in reserve. His settlement cost is only a consequence of transferring the paper to his creditor.

Reserve is often conflated with maturity matching[5]. Management of disparate loan maturities[6] and rates of interest is a risk management strategy. While capital reservation is also a risk management strategy, **the distinction of a reserve is that reserved capital is "present", having a maturity of zero.**

Reference

[1] Chapter: Depreciation Principle
[2] Chapter: Savings Relation
[3] https://en.m.wikipedia.org/wiki/Settlement_(finance)
[4] https://en.m.wikipedia.org/wiki/Gold_certificate
[5] https://en.m.wikipedia.org/wiki/Asset%E2%80%93liability_mismatch
[6] https://en.m.wikipedia.org/wiki/Maturity_(finance)

Risk Free Return Fallacy

The hypothetical concept of risk free rate of return[1] is the economic interest rate obtainable with a guaranteed return of loan principal. There is a theory that Bitcoin allows this to exist in actual practice by enforcing principal return. A corollary to the theory is that this capability can limit credit expansion[2] generally.

The theory requires a provable fixed time covenant[3] on the lent units of coin by the lender. The covenant ensures that the lender cannot spend the units until maturity[4] of the loan and that ownership of the units returns to the lender at that time. The lender trades with a borrower these encumbered units in exchange for interest. The lender's opportunity cost[5] imposed by the covenant is offset by this interest.

However, the units provide no monetary value to the borrower. Full control over the units provably returns to the lender, leaving any person who has accepted them with nothing at that time. **This zero value is necessarily imputed to each exchange prior to maturity and therefore to the loan itself, invalidating the theory.**

There is a related theory that the opportunity cost of the lender can be used to represent a provable expense, just as with proof-of-work. This may be used similarly to hashcash[6] as a way to mitigate denial of service[7]. This is true, however this is an expense and can be achieved by spending (including destroying) units. Just as with proof-of-work, this is a

Reference

[1] https://en.wikipedia.org/wiki/Risk-free_interest_rate
[2] Chapter: Credit Expansion Fallacy
[3] https://en.wikipedia.org/wiki/Covenant_(law)
[4] https://en.wikipedia.org/wiki/Maturity_(finance)
[5] https://en.wikipedia.org/wiki/Opportunity_cost
[6] https://en.wikipedia.org/wiki/Hashcash
[7] https://en.wikipedia.org/wiki/Denial-of-service_attack

trade of provable capital cost for units. As such it does not constitute a loan (i.e. earns no interest), invalidating the theory.

There is a related theory that the units can be used by the borrower to instead track an asset of perpetual value. Given that the tracking expires at maturity, this theory is invalid for the same reason. There is a related theory that the lent units can be used for tracking a fixed-term asset that expires at loan maturity (e.g. a theatre ticket). This is true, however the cost of tracking, for any duration, is limited in BTC by the dust consensus rule to 1 unit. As such the opportunity cost is limited to 1 unit plus at least one transaction fee for establishing 0the loan.

The utility to the borrower is the reduction of the tracking cost over the loan term. At an interest rate of 10% and expiration beyond approximately 7.2 years[1] it becomes cheaper to spend 1 unit than to borrow it. By instead spending just 1 unit outright the asset may be tracked perpetually.

While the final scenario is economically rational, it cannot be accurately described as a loan since the unit can neither be traded nor destroyed by the so-called borrower. It would be more appropriate to refer to this as "rental" of the unit, if only to distinguish it from true lending.

Nevertheless, a return can theoretically be earned on the rental of 1 unit, up to the economic limit imposed by the interest rate (e.g. ~7.2 years at 10%). Yet the fee required for this to be economically rational must be 0 units, as the rental-establishing transaction is required, where it is not when using one's own unit for tracking. So in the case where demand to transact exceeds the fixed confirmation supply, this scenario is not economically rational. This relation holds at any enforced coin dust level above zero to the extent that dust is an insufficient fee to finance confirmation.

Reference

[1] https://en.wikipedia.org/wiki/Rule_of_72

Thin Air Fallacy

There is a theory that fractional reserve banking[1] inherently gives banks the ability to create money at no material cost. The theory does not depend on the state privilege of seigniorage[2]. It is considered a consequence of the accounting practices of free banking[3]. This is sometimes referred to as creating money *ex nihilo* or "out of thin air"[4].

> Banks do not, as too many textbooks still suggest, take deposits of existing money from savers and lend it out to borrowers: they create credit and money ex nihilo – extending a loan to the borrower and simultaneously crediting the borrower's money account.
>
> *Lord Turner, Chairman of the UK Financial Services Authority until its abolition in March 2013*
> *Stockholm School of Economics Conference on: "Towards a Sustainable Financial System"*
> *12 September 2013*

Adherents describe two competing views on money creation. The traditional understanding is naive in relation to their more practical view, as implied by Lord Turner. The theory states that banking inherently creates not only credit, but also money.

Naive View

Money is created by miners at a material cost, potentially sold to people, and eventually lent to people. This theory holds that the lender is lending only money he owns. As such the lender is operating at full reserve[5] and cannot engage in the practice of fractional reserve, which is considered fraudulent. As an honest lender he is only able to issue

Reference

[1] https://en.wikipedia.org/wiki/Fractional-reserve_banking
[2] https://en.wikipedia.org/wiki/Seigniorage
[3] https://en.wikipedia.org/wiki/Free_banking
[4] https://cdn.evbuc.com/eventlogos/67785745/turner.pdf
[5] Chapter: Full Reserve Fallacy

claims (representative money[1]) against money in his possession, preventing credit expansion[2] and therefore persistent price inflation[3].

Practical View

Money substitutes are created by banks, at no material cost, as a consequence of fractional reserve lending. The supply of these substitutes expands with every loan, contracting only as loans are settled[4]. Given the implied lack of constraint on credit expansion, overall debt grows without bound, creating persistent price inflation.

In a free market people can perform the same operations as banks, without necessarily calling themselves banks. Therefore the distinction between these two possibilities must be based on obscuration of the supposed fraud. The theory holds that this obscuration is accomplished using an accounting trick that is not widely understood. So let us investigate the difference. Any money will suffice in this investigation of the money substitutes[5] created in either case, including Gold, Bitcoin or monopoly money[6].

In the naive view, the potential lender has saved both the liquidity required for personal consumption (hoard) and the amount intended for earning interest (investment). All lending in this scenario originates from savings, such as gold accumulated from panning[7]. Savings includes the sum of the hoard (money) and the amount that credit

Reference

[1] https://en.wikipedia.org/wiki/Representative_money
[2] Chapter: Credit Expansion Fallacy
[3] https://en.wikipedia.org/wiki/Inflation
[4] https://en.wikipedia.org/wiki/Clearing_(finance)
[5] https://wiki.mises.org/wiki/Money_substitutes
[6] Chapter: Money Taxonomy
[7] https://en.m.wikipedia.org/wiki/Gold_panning

exceeds debt: savings = money + (credit - debt). Money is gold and credits are money substitutes:

	Savings	Money	Credit	Debt
Person	100oz	100oz		

In this view of personal lending, Person hands over 81oz of gold to Borrower. Borrower accepts an obligation to repay Person with interest at loan maturity[1]. To simplify the accounting we will assume zero interest and no accounting (i.e. discounting) for repayment risk:

	Savings	Money	Credit	Debt
Person	100oz	19oz	81oz	
Borrower		81oz		81oz

Person has actually lent to his own enterprise (e.g. lending business) a fraction of his savings, which is accounted for below. Let us assume that Person hoards 10% of his savings for the liquidity required for near-term consumption and his Business hoards 10% for the same reason:

	Savings	Money	Credit	Debt
Person	100oz	10oz	90oz	
Business		9oz	81oz	90oz
Borrower		81oz		81oz

Person's business is operating with 10% reserve, as 90% of his deposited money is at risk of default. Projecting this into the naive view of banking requires only renaming

Reference

[1] https://en.wikipedia.org/wiki/Maturity_(finance)

"Lender" to "Depositor" and "Business" to "Bank". There is no need to assume that these are distinct individuals:

	Savings	Money	Credit	Debt
Depositor	100oz	10oz	90oz	
Bank		9oz	81oz	90oz
Borrower		81oz		81oz

By properly accounting for Person having money at risk (i.e. a depositor) we can see that all lending is fractionally reserved. There are two loans in this scenario reserved at 10%, resulting in monetary substitutes (credit) of 171% of money. Given the assumption of uniform time preference14, Borrower will lend 90% of his savings, as will all subsequent borrowers. Assuming a minimum practical loan of 1oz, after 43 loans credit expansion terminates at 8.903 times the amount of money.

Where r is the uniform level of individual reserve and m is the amount of money, the total amount of credit c for any number of loans n is given by the following partial sum[1]:

```
c = ∑(n=1..n)[m * (1 - r)^n] =
(m * (r - 1) ((1 - r)^n - 1))/r =
(100oz * (10% - 1) ((1 - 10%)^43 - 1))/10% = 890.3oz
```

The reserve ratio[2] rr is given by the ratio of money to credit:

```
rr = m/c = 100oz/890.3oz = ~11.23%
```

Reference

[1] https://www.wolframalpha.com/input/?i=sum+of+m+*+(1-r)%5En+as+n+goes+from+1+to+infinity

[2] https://en.wikipedia.org/wiki/Reserve_requirement

The money multiplier[1] is given by the inverse of the reserve ratio:

```
1/rr = 1/(100oz/890.3oz) = 8.903
```

It is only because a single dollar is considered the smallest lendable unit that the series is limited to 43 iterations. A continuous function produces a money multiplier of 9 at 10% hoarding.

Iteration yields the following table:

Reference

[1] https://en.wikipedia.org/wiki/Money_multiplier

Loan	Hoarded	Lent	Credit
1	10.00	90.00	90.00
2	19.00	81.00	171.00
3	27.10	72.90	243.90
4	34.39	65.61	309.51
5	40.95	59.05	368.56
6	46.86	53.14	421.70
7	52.17	47.83	469.53
8	56.95	43.05	512.58
9	61.26	38.74	551.32
10	65.13	34.87	586.19
11	68.62	31.38	617.57
12	71.76	28.24	645.81
13	74.58	25.42	671.23
14	77.12	22.88	694.11
15	79.41	20.59	714.70
16	81.47	18.53	733.23
17	83.32	16.68	749.91
18	84.99	15.01	764.91
19	86.49	13.51	778.42
20	87.84	12.16	790.58

21	89.06	10.94	801.52
22	90.15	9.85	811.37
23	91.14	8.86	820.23
24	92.02	7.98	828.21
25	92.82	7.18	835.39
26	93.54	6.46	841.85
27	94.19	5.81	847.67
28	94.77	5.23	852.90
29	95.29	4.71	857.61
30	95.76	4.24	861.85
31	96.18	3.82	865.66
32	96.57	3.43	869.10
33	96.91	3.09	872.19
34	97.22	2.78	874.97
35	97.50	2.50	877.47
36	97.75	2.25	879.72
37	97.97	2.03	881.75
38	98.18	1.82	883.58
39	98.36	1.64	885.22
40	98.52	1.48	886.70
41	98.67	1.33	888.03

| 42 | 98.80 | 1.20 | 889.22 |
| 43 | 98.92 | 1.08 | 890.30 |

Notice that, at full expansion, for any person to spend from his hoard while maintaining his time preference, a loan must be settled to offset the spending. The settlement process moves the money from the former borrower to its lender, and cancels the note. The person in receipt of the spent money must lend it in order to satisfy his time preference, and so on.

No further expansion is possible without an increase in the amount of money or an overall reduction in time preference. An increase in money increases the absolute amount of credit and a reduction in time preference increases the proportion of credit to money. Given that money and credit evolve together, there is never any actual increase in money substitutes apart from these changes.

In the typical practice of bank accounting, Bank does not hand over the money. Instead it creates account entries in a process referred to as "credit creation". It creates offsetting ledger[1] entries for Depositor's proceeds and loan ("credit" and "debt"), and offsetting balance sheet[2] entries for itself ("asset" and "liability"). At the time of loan issuance, the accounts are as follows:

Reference

[1] https://en.wikipedia.org/wiki/Ledger
[2] https://en.wikipedia.org/wiki/Balance_sheet

	Savings	Money	Credit	Debt	Asset	Liability
Depositor	100oz	10oz	90oz		100oz	
Bank		90oz	81oz	171oz	171oz	171oz
Borrower			81oz	81oz	81oz	81oz

This is where explanations of the theory[1] tend to terminate. The offsetting accounts of both Bank and Borrower balance, but Borrower has 81oz of gold to spend, and Bank has not had to turn over any gold to Borrower. There is still only 100oz of money, but Borrower has 81oz of money substitute and Bank has 81oz more in assets. The theory proclaims that Bank has thus created not only credit, but also *money*. Notice that everything still balances, and all accounts can be settled, seemingly validating the theory as espoused by Lord Turner, that "...they create credit and money ex nihilo – extending a loan to the borrower and simultaneously crediting the borrower's money account."

This however demonstrates no actual spending of either the loan credit or the bank asset. Let us take this a bit further by assuming Borrower clears his account, and therefore the corresponding Bank asset and liability entries.

	Savings	Money	Credit	Debt	Asset	Liability
Depositor	100oz	10oz	90oz		100oz	
Bank		9oz	81oz	90oz	90oz	90oz
Borrower		81oz		81oz	81oz	81oz

Notice that the this is identical to the outcome of the naive view. **There is no distinction between these supposedly competing views on money creation**, invaliding the theory.

Reference

[1] https://www.sciencedirect.com/science/article/pii/S1057521915001477

This resolves the centuries-old debate[1], apparently begun between Plato[2] and Aristotle[3], regarding whether money is based on mining or credit. The theories are identical, as money and credit are a duality[4].

> According to Joseph Schumpeter, the first known advocate of a credit theory of money was Plato. Schumpeter describes metallism as the other of "two fundamental theories of money", saying the first known advocate of metallism was Aristotle.

Adherents of the two theories are merely talking past each other[5]. Bitcoin, as fiat (i.e. non-use-value[6] money) without state support[7], has finally made observable both the logical errors of metallism[8], which attempted to show[9] the necessity of use value to money, and chartalism[10], which attempted to show[11] the necessity of state support to fiat.

Recall that each loan is reserved at 10%, so Bank can lend up 8.903 times the amount of money on reserve, or 890.3oz of money substitute against 100oz money reserved. If Bank reserves each loan at 0%, credit expansion would be infinite. However this implies zero time preference, or the idea that time has no value, implying that all money is lent indefinitely. In the case of Bank, 0% reserve implies no liquidity to satisfy any

Reference

[1] https://en.wikipedia.org/wiki/Credit_theory_of_money#Scholarship

[2] https://en.wikipedia.org/wiki/Plato

[3] https://en.wikipedia.org/wiki/Aristotle

[4] https://en.wiktionary.org/wiki/duality

[5] https://en.m.wikipedia.org/wiki/Talking_past_each_other

[6] https://en.m.wikipedia.org/wiki/Use_value

[7] Chapter: Value Proposition

[8] https://en.m.wikipedia.org/wiki/Metallism

[9] Chapter: Regression Fallacy

[10] https://en.m.wikipedia.org/wiki/Chartalism

[11] Chapter: Debt Loop Fallacy

withdrawal (i.e. immediate failure). Yet given zero time preference there could never be any withdrawals, making the scenario irrelevant. Credit expansion is necessarily finite.

So let us revisit the scenario where Bank creates credit at negative reserve (i.e. out of thin air), this time considering spending. For example, on deposits of 0oz Bank intends to issue a loan of 1000oz. Instead of relying on reserved money to eventually settle the loan, Bank "creates money" on its balance sheet. Bank then increases Borrower's credit and debt accounts, representing the borrowed money and the obligation to repay respectively:

	Savings	Money	Credit	Debt	Asset	Liability
Bank			1000oz	1000oz	1000oz	1000oz
Borrower			1000oz	1000oz	1000oz	1000oz

When Borrower trades 1oz (from his credit account) for a car, his credit account is decreased by 1oz and Merchant's is increased by 1oz. Note that Borrower now owes Bank 1oz, as anticipated by the loan agreement.

	Savings	Money	Credit	Debt	Asset	Liability
Bank			1000oz	1000oz	1000oz	1000oz
Borrower	-1oz		999oz	1000oz	999oz	1000oz
Merchant	1oz		1oz		1oz	

All looks good until Merchant attempts to withdraw from his account. At that point Bank has defaulted and Merchant is unpaid. If Merchant's account is with another bank, the payment fails as soon as the two banks attempt to settle accounts. With a hypothetical negative reserve, the accounts balance as follows, indicating Bank's demise[1] (negative money):

	Savings	Money	Credit	Debt	Asset	Liability
Bank	-1oz	-1oz	1000oz	999oz	999oz	999oz
Borrower			999oz	1000oz	999oz	1000oz
Merchant	1oz	1oz			1oz	

The money must actually be moved[2] from the control of Bank to Merchant or Merchant's bank, which is not possible. A simpler example is the failure of any attempt by Borrower to withdraw[3] from his account. Bank may create as much money substitute as it wants, but negative reserve is just an empty promise[4]. In this example Bank has created 1000oz of promises that it cannot keep.

The failure to recognize these principles likely results from failure to consider the settlement process[5]. This likely stems from the failure to recognize the inherent *duality of money and credit*, as the former must always exist to settle the claims implied by the latter. This likely stems from the habit of referring to money (e.g. gold) in the same terms as money substitutes (e.g. credits for gold).

The offsetting asset and liability entries served only to account for loans issued and outstanding, which are the basis of Bank's balance sheet. Bank similarly did not create the offsetting credit and debt entries to obscure fraudulent money creation. Bank created these accounts for two reasons:

Reference

[1] https://en.wikipedia.org/wiki/Bank_failure
[2] https://www.brinks.com/en/public/brinks/logistics
[3] https://en.wikipedia.org/wiki/Automated_teller_machine
[4] https://en.wiktionary.org/wiki/empty_promise
[5] https://www.youtube.com/watch?v=IzE038REw2k

- Preclude physical transfer just to redeposit the money into Bank.

- Encourage redeposit into Bank as opposed to a competitor (or Borrower hoard).

When Bank has insufficient reserve to satisfy withdrawals, either due to loans in default or a bank run[1], it has only two options, default or borrow. To prevent the former, central banking[2] exists to provide the latter. This is the meaning of the term "lender of last resort"[3]. State Banking Principle[4] provides a detailed explanation of this actual source of monetary inflation[5].

In summary, it has been shown that:

- Banks have no ability to create money.

- Fractional reserve is inherent in lending.

- The fraction of reserve is an expression of time preference.

- Zero reserve eliminates any chance of being able to settle accounts.

- No distinction exists between naive and practical theories of money creation.

Reference

[1] https://en.wikipedia.org/wiki/Bank_run
[2] https://en.wikipedia.org/wiki/Central_bank
[3] https://en.wikipedia.org/wiki/Lender_of_last_resort
[4] Chapter: State Banking Principle
[5] https://en.wikipedia.org/wiki/Monetary_inflation

Unlendable Money Fallacy

The Fisher Equation[1] must be used for combining a rate of growth in a money that is itself subject to inflation[2], as depreciation occurs in the future money. This adjusts the nominal interest rate to obtain the real interest rate. Presentation is simplified by using ratios in place of rates. As shown in Depreciation Principle[3], the commodity money growth rate is 0%, or a growth ratio of 100%.

Monopoly money[4] exhibits depreciation due to seigniorage[5].

```
monopoly-money-growth-ratio = commodity-money-growth-ratio / seigniorage-
ratio
100% / 103% = ~97%
```

Fixed supply money may appreciate due to price deflation[6]

```
fixed-supply-money-growth-ratio = commodity-money-growth-ratio / inflation-
ratio
100% / 97% = ~103%
```

A fixed-supply money is presumed to change in purchasing power[7] in proportion to the products it represents (i.e. demand). In other words, with twice the amount of products each unit of the money will trade for twice its previous amount of products.

Reference

[1] https://en.wikipedia.org/wiki/Fisher_equation

[2] https://en.wikipedia.org/wiki/Monetary_inflation

[3] Chapter: Depreciation Principle

[4] Chapter: Money Taxonomy

[5] https://en.wikipedia.org/wiki/Seigniorage

[6] https://en.wikipedia.org/wiki/Deflation

[7] Chapter: Inflation Principle

```
purchasing-power-this-year = purchasing-power-last-year * annual-growth-
ratio
100 * 103% = 103
```

The presumption of fixed-supply money price deflation rests on the assumption of positive economic growth. In the case of economic contraction the money exhibits price inflation[1]. The case of economic growth (increasing wealth) implies interest exceeds depreciation. Both interest and depreciation must always be positive as implied by time preference[2].

```
interest-ratio > depreciation-ratio > 100%
interest-ratio / growth-ratio = depreciation-ratio
interest-ratio / growth-ratio > 100%
interest-ratio > growth-ratio
```

Economic contraction (decreasing wealth) implies an increasing rate of interest, as implied by the theory of marginal utility[3], until positive growth is restored. As such contraction is a self-correcting condition.

```
depreciation-ratio > interest-ratio > 100%
interest-ratio / growth-ratio = depreciation-ratio
interest-ratio / growth-ratio > 100%
interest-ratio > growth-ratio
```

Notice that in both cases of economic growth and contraction, interest must exceed growth, as lending is the only source of growth. Given that growth is the sole basis of deflation in a deflationary money, hoarding the money represents monetary depreciation (consumption).

Reference

[1] https://en.wikipedia.org/wiki/Inflation

[2] Chapter: Time Preference Fallacy

[3] https://en.wikipedia.org/wiki/Marginal_utility

There is a theory that it is economically irrational to lend a deflationary money. **As has been shown, it is rational to lend any money, including one that is deflationary, invalidating the theory.** Any contrary behavior implies a purely speculative condition[1], not supported by the fact of fixed supply.

Reference

[1] Chapter: Speculative Consumption

PRICE

Lunar Fallacy

There is a theory that hoarding bitcoin guarantees to perpetual profit. The theory is based on the following economic laws.

- One money is better than two (Metcalfe's Law[1])
- Better money displaces other monies (Thiers' Law[2])
- At fixed supply, price rises with demand (Law of Supply and Demand[3])
- Potential increase in demand is unbounded (trade is positive sum)

Hoarding is purely speculative, with all returns constituting profit or loss. The money is not lent to another for interest and so is always available for exchange, a benefit that offsets interest forgone.

A corollary to the theory is that no investment in production is required to profit from it. Capital is required for all production. Lenders (investors) earn interest in exchange for time without their capital. **Production is the source of trade and therefore all economic activity results from investment.** A hoard is defined by its lack of consumption in production. If all people hoarded their capital, there would be nothing to trade and therefore no demand for the money.

Reference

[1] https://en.wikipedia.org/wiki/Metcalfe%27s_law
[2] https://en.wikipedia.org/wiki/Gresham%27s_law#Reverse_of_Gresham's_law_(Thiers'_law)
[3] https://en.wikipedia.org/wiki/Supply_and_demand

It seems that the theory is irrational, supporting the idea that Bitcoin is indeed Magic Internet Money[1]. When a theory results in a contradiction, the theory is flawed. A fixed supply market money[2] can only increase in purchasing power due to:

1. economic growth – creating more demand for use of the money is exchange
2. monetization – people transferring demand from another money

Yet economic growth is strictly the result of investment. Growth is necessarily[3] less than the return on investment (interest), and full hoarding is no investment at all. And of course monetization has a limit. Finally, the theory fails to recognize the stability property[4] of Bitcoin. For these reasons the theory is invalid.

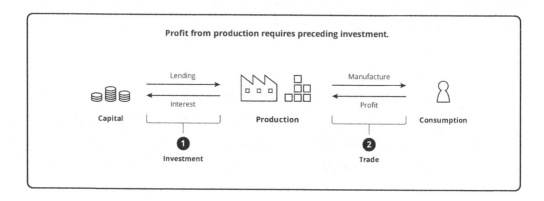

Profit from production requires preceding investment.

Reference

[1] https://medium.com/@paulbars/magic-internet-money-how-a-reddit-ad-made-bitcoin-hit-1000-and-inspired-south-parks-art-b414ec7a5598

[2] Chapter: Money Taxonomy

[3] Chapter: Depreciation Principle

[4] Chapter: Stability Property

Price Estimation

The potential capitalization, and therefore potential unit price, of Bitcoin is estimated in various ways. A common approach is to imagine Bitcoin replacing all state money[1] or even gross world product[2]. Other approaches that use models of past price[3] to predict future price are economically irrational[4] and therefore not considered here. The presumption of Bitcoin as global reserve currency[5] is dismissed for reasons discussed in Reserve Currency Fallacy[6]. The effects of speculative hoarding on price are not considered, based on the Catallactic[7] disproof of speculation as a determinant of price[8].

Given that Bitcoin is money[9] and not credit, the "money" approach is a more rational starting assumption. Yet without a clear understanding of the essential distinction between money and credit, this approach is often flawed in practice. As shown in Credit Expansion Fallacy[10], Bitcoin cannot limit credit expansion. If it eliminated credit expansion (hypothetically), there would be no production whatsoever and it would be worth nothing. The most rational starting assumption regarding credit expansion, is that Bitcoin is reserved at the same rate as other monies. The rate of credit expansion is driven by human time preference[11] alone, so this is an assumption that production is therefore consistent with historical norms.

Reference

[1] https://www.fool.com/investing/2017/05/25/could-the-price-of-bitcoin-go-to-1-million.aspx

[2] https://en.wikipedia.org/wiki/Gross_world_product

[3] https://medium.com/@100trillionUSD/modeling-bitcoins-value-with-scarcity-91fa0fc03e25

[4] Chapter: Stock to Flow Fallacy

[5] Chapter: Reservation Principle

[6] Chapter: Reserve Currency Fallacy

[7] https://en.wikipedia.org/wiki/Catallactics

[8] https://mises.org/library/man-economy-and-state-power-and-market/html/p/949

[9] Chapter: Money Taxonomy

[10] Chapter: Credit Expansion Fallacy

[11] Chapter: Time Preference Fallacy

Let us consider five possible choices for "money" replacement by Bitcoin:

- Tangible money.
- Base money (M0).
- Bank credit (M3-M0).
- All credit (bank, debt, equity).
- Gross product.

Using tangible money ("vault cash") only is an irrational approach. The money that is accounted for as a money equivalent must also be included if one is to consider tangible money, since they are of the same supply. Central banks[1] print and coin tangible money when required, against a base of "obligations" to do so, and all credit in the money is expanded against this base. This concept is discussed in State Banking Principle[2]. Using credit is also an irrational approach, since Bitcoin is not credit. As a money it is used to settle[3] credit obligations. This concept is discussed in Debt Loop Fallacy[4]. So of course using any combination of money and credit (such as M1, M2 or M3[5], as these include M0) is irrational by the same reasoning. Gross product is similarly unjustifiable for substitution as it is neither money nor credit.

However, for the sake of comparison, let us estimate each of the five options listed above. Base values for the following table are U.S. Dollar amounts borrowed from Credit Expansion Fallacy. These are expanded by an estimate of relative size[6] of the world economy by equity market capitalization. The U.S. market is approximately 40% of

Reference

[1] https://en.wikipedia.org/wiki/Central_bank
[2] Chapter: State Banking Principle
[3] https://en.wikipedia.org/wiki/Settlement_(finance)
[4] Chapter: Debt Loop Fallacy
[5] https://en.wikipedia.org/wiki/Money_supply#United_States
[6] https://seekingalpha.com/article/4202768-u-s-percent-world-stock-market-cap-tops-40-percent

global markets. Therefore these values exceed U.S. numbers by a factor of 1/40%. This favors simplicity over precision, as the only objective is to demonstrate a rational method of estimation. The amount of Bitcoin assumed is 18,952,500 given 95% mined (~10 years future) and 5% lost (e.g. Satoshi lost private keys).

Valuations are based on 2019 numbers though Bitcoin inflation is based on 2029. This implies that values should be higher based on the assumption of economic growth and U.S. Dollar monetary inflation[1]. The latter can be eliminated by considering this a constant 2019 dollar projection. Assuming 2% annual real economic growth[2] compounded for 10 years, the 2029 values have been increased by ~22%.

Substitute	Size (2019)	USD/BTC (2029)
Tangible money	$4,347,460,000,000	$279,852
Base Money	$8,187,102,500,000	$527,016
Bank credit	$36,018,735,000,000	$2,318,578
All credit	$236,812,492,891,206	$15,243,965
Gross product	$80,270,000,000,000	$5,167,097

The global base money replacement estimate is $527,016. Determination of net present value[3] requires an estimate of capital cost. Using a conservative value of 7.2% interest implies[4] a 100% opportunity cost[5] of speculation over a ~10 year term, or a present price of $263,508.

Reference

[1] https://en.wikipedia.org/wiki/Monetary_inflation
[2] https://en.wikipedia.org/wiki/Economic_growth
[3] https://en.m.wikipedia.org/wiki/Net_present_value
[4] https://en.m.wikipedia.org/wiki/Rule_of_72
[5] https://en.m.wikipedia.org/wiki/Opportunity_cost

Now we consider the primary assumption, of replacement of all money. Bitcoin offers no security[1] against state prohibition of its use in trade. Under the assumption that states intend to retain seigniorage[2] and censorship, we might multiply by the fraction of the global black market, which is estimated[3] to be ~28% of the global market. The base money estimate includes *all* market activity in the money (credit estimates do not). At 100% replacement for estimated black market trade the price is $73,782.

However given the assumption that state monies are in exclusive use in the white market, we cannot assume 100% of black market activity in Bitcoin. There is no obvious basis for estimating this proportion, but **the 2019 price of ~$10,000 implies a projected 2029 black market adoption of ~7.4%.**

This estimate does not consider the stability property[4] of Bitcoin. It is possible that trade would be forced into monetary substitutes[5] before the currently implied future adoption can be reached.

Reference

[1] Chapter: Permissionless Principle
[2] https://en.wikipedia.org/wiki/Seigniorage
[3] https://voxeu.org/index.php?q=node/7964
[4] Chapter: Stability Property
[5] Chapter: Substitution Principle

Scarcity Fallacy

As an *absolute* concept, economic scarcity[1] of a resource implies only that it is not available in limitless supply. Furthermore, if no person demands even a scarce resource, it has no value. A scarce resource under demand is property. No degree of difficulty in producing the resource is implied.

Scarcity may also refer to the *relative* availability of some property. For a given supply, increasing demand implies decreasing availability (increasing scarcity). However, increasing demand tends to increase production, and thereby availability. Similarly, for a given demand, increasing supply implies increasing availability (decreasing scarcity). However increasing supply tends to decrease production, and thereby availability. These negative feedbacks stabilize availability and correspondingly price.

A single coin has fixed supply[2]. There is a theory that the fixed supply of Bitcoin is the source of its value. As with Bitcoin, there is a fixed supply of the Mona Lisa[3], only one is possible. The theory implies that this is the source of value for the famed work of art. However there are countless unique works of art with no demand, and therefore no value. **Bitcoin cannot increase in value only because of absolute scarcity.** To the contrary, it necessarily becomes more scarce as it becomes more highly valued. Prevalence is not an important monetary property except as it pertains to portability and divisibility.

An aspect of the theory is that Bitcoin's fixed supply is the source of its utility because it ensures non-increasing availability. However, this requires non-decreasing demand. Bitcoin is unique in the realm of property in that the cost of transferring it inherently

Reference

[1] https://en.m.wikipedia.org/wiki/Scarcity
[2] Chapter: Inflation Principle
[3] https://en.m.wikipedia.org/wiki/Mona_Lisa

increases with demand to do so. This effectively creates the same negative demand feedback[1] seen in property without fixed supply.

Unlike the Mona Lisa, it is also subject to effective substitution[2]. Given that non-decreasing demand is not assured the theory is invalid. As is common with economic fallacies, the error stems in part from considering just one side of the supply-demand relation.

Another cause of the error is a misinterpretation of the behavior of commodity monies. Because of its lower prevalence on the surface of the Earth, gold has remained more portable[3] in common scenarios than more prevalent materials such as iron and salt. However the portability of electronic money[4] is independent of the number of units in existence. Apart from sufficient divisibility, the total number of Bitcoin units is entirely arbitrary and therefore unrelated to its utility.

Another cause of the error is a misinterpretation of the behavior of state monies. Through anti-counterfeit laws[5] the state controls the supply of its money by restricting competition. It can therefore collect an inflation tax[6] by expanding supply without consuming as much capital in production, increasing the ratio of money to capital. Without restricted competition supply would expand through market forces, in response to demand, eliminating the tax. In other words the money would behave as a prevalent commodity, with poor portability (at least until remunerated by the state). Poor portability is often an actual consequence of hyperinflation.

Reference

[1] Chapter: Stability Property
[2] Chapter: Substitution Principle
[3] https://en.m.wikipedia.org/wiki/Money#Properties
[4] Chapter: Money Taxonomy
[5] https://en.wikipedia.org/wiki/Counterfeit_money
[6] https://en.m.wikipedia.org/wiki/Seigniorage

Scarcity is a function of both supply and demand and therefore cannot be inherent in a money, even with fixed supply. Both commodity money and Bitcoin eliminate the inflation tax, though commodity money is subject to the negative feedback of monetary inflation and Bitcoin is subject to the negative feedback of fee pressure.

Stability Property

Value is subjective[1] and therefore price constancy is an economic fiction. The exchange prices of a money is determined by its supply and demand[2] which is in turn affected by the demand schedules of all people for all products. The stability of a money is not a tendency toward constant price in all other things, it is a damping[3] relationship between demand for the money and its supply.

We can organize monies into three supply categories:

- Market supply (commodity[4])
- Monopoly supply (monopoly[5])
- Fixed supply (bitcoin[6])

In any money, destruction of units decreases supply and therefore increases the value of those that remain. Given that there is no financial incentive for loss it does not impact stability.

Commodity money supply increases due to the financial incentive to produce more[7] when price is expected to be at or above production cost (inclusive of capital cost). This relationship between price and supply is predictable despite price (and therefore supply) not being so Competition ensures that this production, financed by existing owners, is

Reference

[1] https://en.wikipedia.org/wiki/Subjective_theory_of_value

[2] https://en.m.wikipedia.org/wiki/Supply_and_demand

[3] https://en.wikipedia.org/wiki/Damping_ratio

[4] https://en.wikipedia.org/wiki/Commodity

[5] Chapter: Money Taxonomy

[6] https://en.wikipedia.org/wiki/Bitcoin

[7] https://en.m.wikipedia.org/wiki/Gold_mining

limited by current price. The feedback of value decrease resulting from supply increase reduces production incentive, creating stability.

Monopoly money supply is increased arbitrarily (or taxed as demurrage[1]) by the sovereign[2] due to the financial reward of seigniorage[3].

When this monetary inflation is predictable it can be capitalized, which discounts the return on seigniorage. As such changes to supply are often not published[4]. Due to state monopoly[5] protection (i.e. production is the crime of counterfeit), competition cannot effectively limit returns. The resulting sovereign profit (tax) is the reward of seigniorage and the reason for monopoly money[6]. Monopoly protection is the sole economic distinction between commodity and monopoly money. The supply increase caused by seigniorage is mitigated only by political unrest as people resist the consequential value decrease. This unrest initially manifests as capital flight[7], which is countered by foreign exchange controls[8].

As fees necessarily rise with demand the utility threshold[9] eliminates demand for transaction of value below the threshold. More generally, the fee level rises to the point where monetary substitutes[10] are more cost-effective for a given value transaction. **Stability therefore results from limiting demand directly, in contrast to relying on an**

Reference

[1] https://en.wikipedia.org/wiki/Demurrage_(currency)

[2] https://en.wikipedia.org/wiki/Sovereignty

[3] https://en.wikipedia.org/wiki/Seigniorage

[4] https://www.reuters.com/article/us-venezuela-economy/crisis-hit-venezuela-halts-publication-of-another-major-indicator-idUSKBN16S1YF

[5] https://en.wikipedia.org/wiki/State_monopoly

[6] Chapter: Reservation Principle

[7] https://en.wikipedia.org/wiki/Capital_flight

[8] https://en.wikipedia.org/wiki/Foreign_exchange_controls

[9] Chapter: Utility Threshold Property

[10] Chapter: Substitution Principle

increase in supply to do so. Stability implies that price is bounded, yet it can rise with increased effective transaction carrying capacity[1] of the coin, and with increased utility relative to substitutes.

Reference

[1] Chapter: Scalability Principle

Stock to Flow Fallacy

Stock-to-Flow[1] historically describes the relationship between capital and income, allowing a future capital level to be estimated from an expected income level. Later this elemental concept was applied to money supply generally.

The ratio of stock to flow is a measure of time. Given a higher ratio, stock will increase more slowly. There is a theory that money with a higher inherent stock-to-flow ratio will suffer less proportional monetary inflation[2] than a money with a lower ratio. The theory holds that the higher ratio implies a "harder" money, defined as inherently more resistant to the effects of monetary inflation.

The theory fails to consider the source of flow rates. It necessarily assumes that the rate of production is simply a property of the substance. But production of anything occurs when the anticipated price makes production profitable. A greater profit potential results in more competition, accelerating supply increase. More people digging for gold increases its flow.

In other words, flow is a function of demand. An anticipated loss results in no production whatsoever. This lack of any flow is *not inherent in the substance* but a consequence of *lack of demand*. Given that both supply and demand determine flow, the theory is invalid. This long understood[3] error is not an aspect of the elemental stock-to-flow concept, but a misapplication of it.

Given counterfeit laws, competition to produce state money is restricted, allowing control of supply by the state, independent of market forces. As with other monies,

Reference

[1] https://en.m.wikipedia.org/wiki/Stock_and_flow
[2] https://en.m.wikipedia.org/wiki/Monetary_inflation
[3] https://mises.org/library/theory-money-and-credit/html/ppp/1234

supply and demand are generally unpredictable. A state may "peg" its issue of reserve notes[1] to another money, such as gold. This relation may even hold over many decades. In this case the stock-to-flow ratio would incorrectly indicate a "hardness" comparable to that of gold.

Given that the stock-to-flow of money is the inverted monetary inflation rate, its relationship with monetary inflation is tautological. It does not imply anything about future monetary inflation. It can be used to analyze historical relations, and to calculate future stock based on *assumed* future flow, but it cannot be used to *predict* future monetary inflation. Any statement that one speculation will be more profitable than another based on historical stock-to-flow ratios is an error.

Reference

[1] Chapter: Reservation Principle

SCALABILITY

Auditability Fallacy

Solvency of a Bitcoin custodian cannot be audited. A custodian is a person with discretion both in the release of an asset and issuance of securities against it. If both release of the asset and the issuance of securities against it are controlled by consensus rules, then the relationship is not actually custodial. This is the distinction between a reserve[1] and a layer. A layer is protocol-enforced (non-custodial) and therefore has nothing to audit.

A solvency audit requires simultaneous (atomic) proof of both the full amount of the asset held by a custodian and the securities issued against it. In the case of a national Bitcoin reserve this would require complete proof of all fiat (e.g. the security) issued against the reserve, as well as the Bitcoin held in reserve. Even in the case where the security is issued on a distinct public chain the atomicity requirement is not satisfied.

In some cases it may be considered sufficient to waive the atomicity requirement, accepting incorrectness under the assumption that material deviation would eventually be discovered. However in the case of state banking[2] it is insufficient to detect the deviation. Historically it has not been difficult to detect such deviations. The difficulty arises in stopping them.

Reference

[1] Chapter: Reservation Principle
[2] Chapter: Reserve Currency Fallacy

Scalability Principle

Scalability[1] is the proportional increase in some aspect of performance as more hardware is employed. Bitcoin transaction throughput is perfectly non-scalable as no amount of hardware increases it.

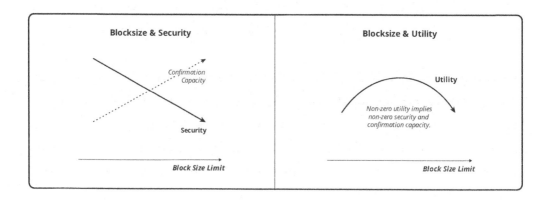

The block size limit consensus rule establishes the arbitrary trade-off between utility and system security. Increased block size marginally increases transaction throughput and therefore the resource cost of transaction validation (i.e. processing, storage, and bandwidth). As the cost of validation increases, economic security is adversely impacted by increased centralization risk[2]. As the trade-off is arbitrary, there is no ideal size.

Reference

[1] https://en.wikipedia.org/wiki/Scalability

[2] Chapter: Centralization Risk

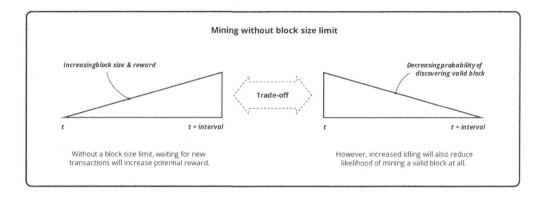

At any block size the system remains non-scalable due to the necessity of confirmation finality. A finite set of transactions must be selected, which implies that others may be excluded. This exclusion is financially motivated by the opportunity cost[1] of not utilizing deployed mining capital, and is the manifestation of non-scalability. This inherent limit necessitates a competitive market for confirmation, and finances it in proportion to demand for the money[2].

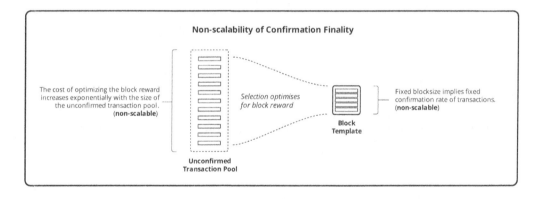

Effective transaction carrying capacity, and therefore utility, can be increased by layering. This represents a *local* and *time-limited* security compromise, in contrast to the *system-wide* and *persistent* security compromise of increasing block size.

Reference

[1] https://en.wikipedia.org/wiki/Opportunity_cost

[2] Chapter: Money Taxonomy

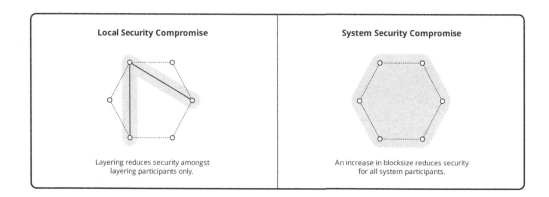

Either compromise lowers but does not eliminate the utility threshold[1], which implies the stability property[2] is preserved.

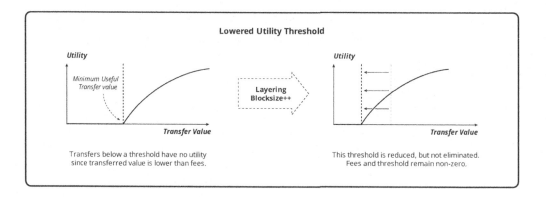

Therefore stability and non-scalability exist at any block size and level of layering.

Reference

[1] Chapter: Utility Threshold Property

[2] Chapter: Stability Property

Substitution Principle

A substitute good[1] is one that can be used in place of another. As the price of a product rises, at some level people either move to substitutes or cease use altogether.

While a substitute would be less desirable at the same price as the original product, its lower price offsets this preference. In this manner the presence of substitutes reduces demand for the original good. The substitute competes with the original just as does increased supply of the original.

Given that a coin has fixed supply, it is commonly assumed that no supply side increase can reduce upward price pressure. As shown in Stability Property[2], Bitcoin integrates transfer fees which necessarily rise with use. This unique characteristic creates downward price pressure by reducing demand. **But this rising cost also makes substitutes viable, creating downward price pressure by effectively increasing supply.**

There is nothing preventing the evolution of multiple similar coins. It is possible for these to exhibit nearly indistinguishable monetary properties, minimizing the substitution trade-off. As shown in Consolidation Principle[3], there is always pressure toward a single money, as this eliminates the exchange cost. However this pressure is at odds with rising costs, and at some level of use must give way to substitution (or disuse).

There is a theory that since creation of new coins costs nothing, the substitution principle implies that Bitcoin must become worthless due to unlimited free supply. This

Reference

[1] https://en.m.wikipedia.org/wiki/Substitute_good
[2] Chapter: Stability Property
[3] Chapter: Consolidation Principle

ignores the fact that Bitcoin requires people pay to use it. This is as true for a second coin as it is for the first.

And increasing supply relieves demand. At some point demand is not sufficient to produce/secure more supply, and as such the theory is invalid. This is the same relationship that holds with commodity monies and indeed all products.

Utility Threshold Property

Utility is expressed as preference for the coin over substitutes, for transfers of a comparable value. Increasing utility implies a rising fee level, given the presumption of increasing transaction volume. Competition for confirmation bids up fees. Given differences in the market fee price over time, one may offer an uncompetitive fee in expectation of a longer time to confirm. Others will not transact on the chain, relying instead on substitutes.

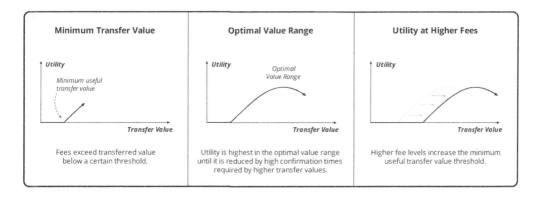

Minimum Transfer Value	Optimal Value Range	Utility at Higher Fees
Fees exceed transferred value below a certain threshold.	Utility is highest in the optimal value range until it is reduced by high confirmation times required by higher transfer values.	Higher fee levels increase the minimum useful transfer value threshold.

Increasing utility therefore implies increasing average transfer value, as rising fees will otherwise cause the cost of transfer to exceed the value transferred. Greater depth implies greater confirmation security. Therefore time can be traded for *higher* security against double-spend. However time cannot be reduced below one block period to achieve *lower* security. The lowest levels of security are none (unconfirmed) and minimal (one confirmation). There is no trade to be made between these levels.

Higher fees imply higher hash rate cost mitigating the need to increase confirmation depth for higher value transfers. **But given there is no way to reduce security for lower value transfers, the useful minimum value transfer rises with utility.** Failure to support transfers in a certain value range implies substitutes are cheaper in that range.

This implies the possibility of coexisting moneys to service distinct value ranges. However all Bitcoins[1] inherently exhibit this property.

Rule differences in terms of block period or size do not change this relationship. The effect of these coin variations is strictly proportional. Even unlimited size blocks must produce fee levels that price out low value transfers.

Reference

[1] Chapter: Bitcoin Labels

APPENDIX

Glossary of Terms

Activation

Starting to Enforce a new Rule.

Adjustment

A change to Difficulty.

Aggregation

The tendency toward reduced participation in Mining or Validation. Implies Pooling or Centralization.

Announcement

The first Communication of a Block to another Person.

Apparent Hash Power

A fraction of Blocks in a Chain Segment. Public estimates of specific Miner Hash Power are based on this.

Attack

Use of Hash Power to enable Double-Spending.

Bitcoin

The set of principles that secure a Coin from the State. The term and principles are defined by Satoshi in "Bitcoin: A Peer-to-Peer Electronic Cash System".

Block

A Valid set of Transactions with Timestamp and Proof.

Block Pool

The set of Weak Blocks. Orphan Pool is a misnomer for this.

Borrow

To Trade time with Units for property of greater Utility to the Lender.

Branch

A Valid sequence of Blocks.

Candidate

A potential Block with undetermined Proof.

Cap

The limit to Supply over all time.

Capitalization

The product of Price and Supply.

Censorship

Subjective Confirmation.

Centralization

The tendency toward few Merchants. Merchants directly control Validation. May also refer to Pooling.

Chain

The Branch with the most cumulative Proof.

Claimant

A Person who holds a claim on property under the control of a Custodian. Also, a lien-holder, shareholder, lender, or depositor.

Client-Server

An asymmetrical Protocol.

Coercion

Use of aggression to compel Activation.

Coin

A Consensus regarding a mutually acceptable medium for Trade. BTC is a Coin.

Coinbase

A Transaction that Transfers a Reward.

Communication

Conveyance of data between Machines.

Confirmation

Inclusion of a Transaction in a Block.

Consensus

An agreement among People. Also, the set of people who participate in an agreement.

Consensus Rules

The set of constraints that define a Coin.

Contract

A Script that expresses Transfer conditions. Public Key Script is an anachronism for this.

Co-option

Use of aggression to control Hash Power.

Correlation

The ability to Taint using statistical Chain analysis.

Custodian

A Person who controls the property of another by agreement.

Decentralization

The tendency opposing Centralization.

Decouple

A Mine that shares Reward with another to reduce Variance.

Delegation

The tendency toward few Owners. Owners directly control Spending.

Denial of Service

Using Communication to exploit Protocol or Implementation flaws that degrade performance. DoS is an acronym for this.

Depth

One more than the count of Blocks after a Confirmation.

Developer

A Person creating an Implementation.

Difficulty

The level of Proof required for Validity.

Distortion

Market aggression that skews the cost of Mining.

Double-Spend

The Endorsement of the same Output Contract by distinct Spends.

Dust

An insufficient number of Units for Transfer via an Output. BTC Consensus Rules prohibit transfer of less than one unit.

Economic Power

A fraction of all property offered in Exchange.

Economy

The set of all Merchants.

Endorsement

A Script that satisfies a Contract. Signature Script is an anachronism for this.

Enforcement

The act of discarding Invalid data.

Exchange

The Trade of Units for other property.

Fee

An implicit Transfer to a Miner.

Fork

A divergence in Consensus Rules.

Genesis

The first Block of all Branches of a Coin.

Grind

A Tool that performs Hashing.

Grinder

A Person operating a Grind.

Halving

A reduction in the Subsidy rate (by half).

Hard Fork

A Fork that implies a Split. Expansion of the set of potentially-Valid Blocks.

Hash

An atomic computation to Prove Candidate Validity.

Hash Power

A fraction of the Hash Rate of all Mines.

Hash Rate

The rate of Hashing.

Height

The count of preceding Blocks in a Branch.

Hoard

To Own for future use.

Honest

A Miner who builds on the Blocks of others.

Identity

The means to associate Communication with a Person.

Implementation

A specific Tool set.

Inflation

The increase in Supply resulting from Subsidy. A monetary inflation, not to be confused with Price Inflation.

Input

An Output Point and an Endorsement.

Interest

The rate of increase in Utility from Lending.

Latency

The delay inherent in Communication.

Layering

Trade using a sequence of Unconfirmed Transactions that can be Settled by either party.

Lend

To Trade time without Units for property of greater Utility. Invest is an alias for this.

Locktime

An expression of earliest Transaction Validity.

Loss

Failure of Investment to earn the Market rate of Interest.

Machine

An instruction follower.

Majority Hash Power

A subset of Miners with sufficient Hash Power to execute a sustained Attack. 51% is a common approximation of sufficient power.

Market

The Trade in certain property.

Maturity

The Depth at which a Coinbase Output becomes Transferable.

Median Time Past

An average of preceding Block Timestamps.

Merchant

A Person accepting Units in Trade. User is a common alias for this.

Mine

A Tool that performs Work.

Miner

A Person operating a Mine.

Node

A Tool that performs Validation.

Operation

An atomic declaration of intent.

Optimization

A Tool change that reduces the cost of Mining.

Organization

An Announcement adding a Block to the Chain.

Output

An explicit Transfer and a Contract.

Owner

A Person controlling certain Units. Holder is a common alias for this.

Partition

An inability of certain Nodes to Communicate.

Partitioning

The tendency toward persistent Partitions.

Peer-to-Peer

A symmetrical Protocol.

Period

The average time between Organizations.

Person

A decision maker.

Point

A reference to an Output or Input.

Political

Pertaining to the actions of States.

Pooling

The tendency toward few Miners, including consolidation by Relays.

Power

The relative level of control of a Person over the Chain or Coin.

Previous Output

The Output to which an Input refers.

Price

An average or instantaneous Exchange rate.

Price Inflation

The increase in Price over time.

Profit

A return on Investment above the Market rate of Interest.

Proof

Valid evidence.

Proof-of-Memory

Probabilistic Proof of an amount of usable computing memory (PoM).

Proof-Of-Stake

Cryptographic Proof of an amount of Ownership (PoS).

Proof-Of-Work

Probabilistic Proof of an amount of Work performed (PoW).

Protocol

A set of Communication conventions.

Relay

A Tool that disseminates new Blocks.

Relayer

A Person operating a Relay.

Reorganization

An Announcement promoting a Weak Branch to the Chain. Reorg is an abbreviation for this.

Reward

The sum of Subsidy and Fees for a Block.

Rule

A subset of Consensus Rules.

Script

A set of Operations that authorizes Transfer.

Segment

A contiguous subset of a Branch.

Selfish

A Miner who is not being Honest.

Settlement

Confirmation of Layered Transactions.

Signal

A Miner indication via Block data of intent to Enforce a new Rule.

Soft Fork

A Fork that implies a Split unless Enforced by Majority Hash Power. Contraction of the set of potentially-Valid Blocks.

Speculate

To Own in expectation of Price increase. Also to Borrow in expectation of price decrease.

Spend

The initial publication of a Transaction.

Split

A Coin bifurcation.

Stall

The lack of Height increase over time.

State

A set of People that uses aggression in place of Trade. Typically operates with impunity within geographic limits.

Strong

A Branch with more cumulative Proof than another.

Subsidy

The issuance of new Units to a Miner.

Supply

The set of all issued Units.

Taint

Determination of Ownership.

Timestamp

A declaration of the time of Block production.

Tool

A set of Machine instructions.

Trade

A voluntary swap of property between two People.

Transaction

A Valid record of Transfer.

Transaction Pool

The set of Unconfirmed Transactions. Memory Pool is a misnomer for this.

Transfer

The change of control over certain Units.

Unconfirmed

A Transaction that does not exist in a Block on the Chain.

Unit

A minimum Transferable amount of property represented by a Coin. The satoshi is the Bitcoin unit.

Utility

The usefulness of certain property to a Person.

Validation

The process of determining Validity.

Validity

Conformance to Consensus Rules.

Value

The preference of a Person for certain property over other.

Variance

The varying frequency of achieving a Reward.

Variation

Differences in the resource cost of Mining.

Volatility

Deviation in Price over time.

Wallet

A Tool that creates Transactions.

Weak

A Branch with less cumulative Proof than another. Orphan is a misnomer for this.

Withholding

The purposeful delay of Announcement.

Work

The process of Block production.

Made in the USA
Coppell, TX
02 November 2021

65083110R00181

CRYPTOECONOMICS

Fundamental Principles of Bitcoin

Eric Voskuil